FAMILY AND LIFE

FAMILY AND LIFE

POPE FRANCIS

PASTORAL REFLECTIONS

FROM HIS YEARS AS
ARCHBISHOP OF BUENOS AIRES, 1998–2013

THE PONTIFICAL COUNCIL FOR THE FAMILY
PAULIST PRESS
New York / Mahwah, New Jersey
WILLIAM H. SADLIER, INC.

BX
1378.7
·A25
2015

Library of Congress Control Number: 2015931782
ISBN 978-0-8091-4946-9 (Paulist Press paperback)
ISBN 978-1-58768-546-0 (Paulist Press e-book)
ISBN 978-0-8215-3022-1 (William H. Sadlier, Inc. paperback)
ISBN 978-0-8215-3025-2 (William H. Sadlier, Inc. e-book)

Published by
William H. Sadlier, Inc.
9 Pine Street
New York, NY 10005-4700
www.sadlier.com
and
Paulist Press
997 Macarthur Boulevard
Mahwah, New Jersey 07430-2045
www.paulistpress.com

Printed and bound in the United States of America

CONTENTS

SELECTED CHAPTERS

of

*Las Enseñanzas de Jorge Mario Bergoglio Papa Francisco Sobre La Familia y La Vida, 1999-2013**

that are included in this volume:

*The English translation of the title is *The Teachings of Jorge Mario Bergoglio Pope Francis on the Family and Life, 1999-2013,* Special Issue of the periodical *Familia et Vita, Edición Española, Libreria Editrice Vaticana (2013).*

ABBREVIATIONS USED IN THIS VOLUME

FOREWORD

Three significant family-related events are making the time between October 2014 and October 2015 particularly important for the Universal Church: in Rome, a Meeting of the Synod of Bishops dealing with the family was held in October 2014; in the United States, the Eighth World Meeting of Families in Philadelphia, Pennsylvania, will be held in September 2015, sponsored by the Pontifical Council for the Family; and, again in Rome, in October 2015, a second Meeting of the Synod of Bishops will be held dealing with the family.

In support of these events, which are of great importance for the Church's evangelizing mission, the Pontifical Council for the Family has gathered and translated into English fifteen documents on the subjects of Holy Matrimony, the family, and life, which Pope Francis, as Cardinal Jorge Mario Bergoglio, wrote when he was Archbishop of Buenos Aires (1998–2013).

It is our hope that with this volume our Holy Father, whose pastoral energy and intellectual depth have long been appreciated in his native Argentina and in Latin America, will become even more widely known and loved in the English-speaking world.

What he wrote makes plain his pastoral wisdom and the evangelical love he showed for the family and for life during the years of his episcopal ministry in Buenos Aires, and in the Episcopal Council of Latin America and the Caribbean.[1]

With the help of the Institute for Marriage and the Family of the Pontifical Catholic University of Argentina in Buenos Aires, which deserves heartfelt thanks for its significant assistance; and with the contribution of Rev. José Guillermo Gutiérrez Fernández,

---

[1] Referred to in this volume as "CELAM."

an Official of our Council, and of our valued friend and collaborator James M. Crowley, who oversaw this translation and its publication, we have studied the theological, pastoral and cultural thinking of Cardinal Bergoglio, and we recognize in him *sapientia cordis*, "wisdom of the heart," that is supported by a real-world understanding of the problems that challenge individuals, families, the Church, and the postmodern world today.

In preparing this material, we were first struck by the style and directness of the Cardinal's thought, which has happily remained unchanged after his election to the See of Peter. Pope Francis speaks just as Cardinal Bergoglio did in Buenos Aires, communicating concepts with an immediacy and directness that make the heart see, that rouse sleeping consciences, and that challenge the intelligence. His cultural communication process starts from the heart to challenge the conscience, then enlivens the intelligence and reason.

When Cardinal Bergoglio spoke to his people, it was a pleasure to listen to him. He used brief phrases (at times a little sharp), quotations that were appropriate and imaginative, and a simple, convincing manner of speaking. He is also expert at adjusting his style of delivery to the occasion and his listeners.

The texts that we included in this edition all have Holy Matrimony, the family and life as their basic themes, but they always deal with those themes in the context of everyday realities, never in the abstract. Throughout, however, there is one guiding light that helps the reader better understand the Cardinal's wide-ranging thought: the *Aparecida Document*,[2] that is, the Concluding Report of the Fifth General Conference of the Bishops of Latin

---

[2]   Cited in this volume as "AD" and available online at http://www.celam.org/aparecida/ingles.pdf

America and the Caribbean, which was held at the Shrine of Aparecida in Brazil in 2007.[3] The Cardinal was one of the principal authors of the document, and he refers to it often in the following chapters, something he also did as Pope during the 2013 World Youth Day in Rio de Janeiro.

With respect to the *Aparecida Document*, it is a pleasure to note that before being elected Pope, Cardinal Bergoglio was a member of the Presidential Committee of our Council, and when his friend, the former President of the Council, Cardinal Alfonso López Trujillo, died, we asked His Eminence to prepare a commemorative lecture in the late Cardinal's honor. It is entitled *The Family in the Light of the Aparecida Document*,[4] and it is reproduced as the first chapter of this volume. It deals with many family issues, but it addresses in particular an aspect of family life that Pope Francis has spoken about often and in depth during his pontificate: the relationship in the family between children and the elderly. In that 2008 document, Cardinal Bergoglio wrote, "We have to recognize that every boy or girl who is marginalized, abandoned or living on the streets, with scant access to education and healthcare, is a living example not only of injustice but also of the breakdown of institutions—the family and its neighborhood network, local charities, the parish, and all the different government agencies." He continues, noting that at the other end of life we see the elderly, who are "repositories of the collective memory of the nation and the family.... The family is the place where the elderly are welcome and supported. And the Church celebrates the gift that the elderly are in so many parish communities." The *Aparecida Document* shows Cardinal

---

[3] The meeting is referred to in this volume as the "Aparecida Conference."

[4] First published in *Familia et Vita*, XIII, 2-3/2008, pp. 64-72.

Bergoglio's ability to get to the heart of the matter, as when he says that society must support "caring and fair policies that make our elderly full members of society and not simply recipients of politically-motivated handouts. What's needed is a community where all are welcome, rather than isolated facilities where the elderly can live without bothering us.... The elderly are disciples and missionaries with a specific vocation: to be models of good sense and maturity for younger generations—teachers of prayer and, at the same time, teachers of generous commitment."

It is enough to look at the table of contents of this volume to appreciate the relevance and value of what the Cardinal presents. We recognize themes that recur frequently in the daily preaching of Pope Francis, preaching that is both Gospel-centered and Franciscan: the culture of dialogue and of encounter, care for others, the school as a place of warm welcome, the urgency of redirecting politics toward greater creativity, the opening of hearts to fill them with hope. He speaks as well of the inculturation of the Gospel, of social and family solidarity, of the family and the parish, and of the real dangers that children and teenagers must face. He does not shy away from socially sensitive issues: euthanasia, abortion, divorce, same-sex marriage, human trafficking and slavery. There is also a strong Marian element in his reflections, as when he speaks of Our Lady of Luján, the Patroness of Argentina, whose devoted children look to her with affection and grateful hearts, or when he speaks of her love and care for those who are suffering, of her care for life itself.

The documents in this volume were originally written or delivered in Spanish or Italian, and the Council published them in a two-volume Spanish and Italian edition in 2013. Now, in the preparation of this English-language edition we are grateful for the cooperation of the William H. Sadlier, Inc. publishing company of

New York City and the Paulist Press of Mahwah, New Jersey (which is one of the mission activities of the Paulist Fathers, an American Society of Apostolic Life). We are also grateful to Father Christopher Gibson, C.P., a one-time student of the then-younger Jesuit Jorge Bergoglio in Buenos Aires, for his work on this translation; and to Bernard F. Stehle, a professor at Community College of Philadelphia, for his editing assistance.

In this volume, at the beginning of each chapter, we have inserted a footnote that gives information about the source of the material that makes up the chapter.

More generally, I would like to note that this volume is not the Council's first presentation of this type. In early 2013, we published a Special Issue of *Familia et Vita*[5] dedicated to "Family and Life in the Teaching of Benedict XVI," and we recommend it as a way to appreciate the continuity and consistency of the Church's teaching about the Gospel of the Family.

We hope, as this important year proceeds, that it will be both useful and worthwhile for the reader to see how the thoughts of Cardinal Bergoglio presage those of Pope Francis, who is working, with the grace and strength of his Petrine Office, to show the world the beauty of the family as the basic cell of society and as a reflection of the Trinitarian mystery of our loving God.

Rev. Gianfranco Grieco, O.F.M. Conv.
Office Director, Pontifical Council for the Family
Director, *Familia et Vita*

March 1, 2015

---

[5] XVIII, 1-2/2013.

INTRODUCTION
THE FAMILY AND LIFE:
TWO CONSTANTS THAT BUILD THE FUTURE

Archbishop Vincenzo Paglia
President of the Pontifical Council for the Family

A number of the homilies, lectures, reports, and other documents that Pope Francis authored when he was Archbishop of Buenos Aires, and that are collected in this volume, were provided to the Synod Fathers at the October 2014 Extraordinary Synod on the Family to help show them how the Holy Father's understanding of the family has developed and how it is part of his larger vision of society as a whole. It is our hope that this volume will be similarly, and particularly, useful to persons who seek to follow the guidance presented in the Pope's Apostolic Exhortation *Evangelii Gaudium*, especially the participants in the September 2015 World Meeting of Families in Philadelphia, and those who take part in, or who follow, the discussions and conclusions of the meeting of the Synod of Bishops on the Family in Rome in October of 2015.

We further hope that these chapters, which show the Holy Father's broad understanding of global realities affecting the family and life, will be of value to all people of good will throughout the English-speaking world. Here we think especially those government officials and world leaders whom he will meet and who will listen to his words as he travels the world in fulfillment of his Apostolic mission.

For Cardinal Bergoglio, the family was a concrete and human reality, the place to learn the art of living and loving. The family is made up of faces: of persons who love, who speak, who sacrifice themselves for others and defend life at all costs. One becomes a person by being in a family, by growing up with one's parents, by breathing in the warmth of the home. Here we are given our name and therefore our dignity; here we learn about friendship, we experience affection, we taste intimacy; here we learn the art of dialogue and interpersonal communication.

The Cardinal's short talks, homilies, and reflections about the family evoke the sweet lullabies that grandmothers sing to their grandchildren. They allow the reader to imagine the lined faces of elderly souls, worn out by their sacrifices but kept happy by love for their children. They make us remember the long-ago noise of children playing and singing in the backyards near their homes and in the open air. These are vivid images of the family and its members who represent a link in the long chain that is life.

Likewise, he speaks of Holy Matrimony, which was part of God's plan from the beginning and is the foundation of the family because Holy Matrimony is a step in the process of "humanization" of the individual and the world. Holy Matrimony is like a "first Sacrament" of humankind, where the individual discovers him or herself and understands him or herself in relation to another, and to others, and to the love that is able to receive love and return it.

The Cardinal believed that without this basic anthropological fact it is not possible to begin any theological reflection about the value and meaning of the family and of life itself. In addition, he believed that without studying families in their own situations[6] and

---

[6] As an example of context, and aware of the difficult life situations that many families in Latin America face, Cardinal Bergoglio pointed out especially: poverty and need in many families; emigration made necessary by lack of employment opportunities and by violence in many regions of Latin America; violence that destroys family bonds; the growing phenomenon of sexual abuse within families; divorce viewed as a legal right; anti-life campaigns that are spreading in many

carefully analyzing the social, economic, political, cultural, and religious conditions in which life is lived, every other speculation—even philosophical or sacramental—would be pointless, ineffective. In some way, every one of us is born—is delivered into the world—through circumstances that reflect, however dimly, or even negatively, God's plan for the family and for that spousal love that receives sacramental dignity in Holy Matrimony.

1. Two Forces at Work

In the teaching of Cardinal Bergoglio, particularly as his thought is reflected in the *Aparecida Document*, the family is subject to two forces that interact with and sustain each other.

The first is life. It draws all things to itself but in turn everything flows from it as from a great and inexhaustible flood that washes its waters up in roiling waves that eventually reach even the most tranquil streams. The flow of life carries us from generation to generation. All are part of a "family of families," where memory—which is necessary to ensure a truly human future—is the treasure of the elderly and is received gratefully by younger generations as they learn the joy that comes from relationships and from human communion.

The second is love as the gift of self. It is a flame that the more it burns, the more it renews itself and finds new strength and brilliance. Love creates the person, brings each of us into being.

a) The Energy of Life

With the words "force" or "energy" of life, Pope Francis isn't referring simply to the mark that every person leaves in time and

communities with the help of the media and legislation; abandonment of the elderly, and the exploitation of minors.

in history just by reason of his or her existence. "Life" is not to be equated with simple "*bíos*" but rather with "*zōē*"[7]—which is an intergenerational force that crosses time, history (starting from what is both the source of life and our final home, the "bosom of Abraham"), societies, and civilizations, and that renews itself when communities and peoples open themselves to the gift of love and know how to treasure their own memories.[8]   Even if it were possible, it would be an oversimplification to reread the role of the family and the meaning of the individual existence only in the "pop culture" framework of one's own "biography" or "generation." When Cardinal Bergoglio envisioned the family, he saw very specific faces: grandparents, young people, adults and children, who, with their being and their action, make up community and nourish humanity and constitute the holy People of God, whose father is Abraham.

On many occasions, the Archbishop recalled that in each one of us there is more than our own personal "life story" and more than the few and fading traces that our own families and communities leave. Each one of us is tied to a divine origin that precedes us and

---

[7] See Chapter One below, where Cardinal Bergoglio speaks of the family as the "patrimony of humanity and wealth of our peoples" and of the "culture of life and protection of the environment."

[8] See Chapter Six below. In a conference organized by the Christian Association of Entrepreneurs on September 1, 1999, "Education and Encounter," Cardinal Bergoglio, speaking of life, made reference to the memory of a people (Argentinians, for example) saying that it cannot be reduced to a simple chronicle. Every people must have in its historical, spiritual, and cultural memory the awareness of its own dignity. In that context Cardinal Bergoglio spoke of "embers of memory" that hold, like coals hold fire, the values that make us great: how we celebrate and defend life, how we accept death, how we care for the weaknesses of the poorest of our brothers and sisters, how we open our hands to solidarity when faced with suffering and poverty, how we enjoy ourselves, and how we pray.

that we know is waiting for us as our eternal home, the goal of our time on Earth. It is the divine life in which every human person, from generation to generation, first shares at the unique moment of his or her conception and thereafter in his or her own life with others.[9]

We are all like links in the chain of time that carries from generation to generation the values, the ideals, and the acts of love and tenderness that every people can perform along humanity's unique and multifaceted journey.

In this light, we can better understand an expression that appeared again and again in what Pope Francis preached when he was Archbishop of Buenos Aires: "Caring for" or "taking care of" life at every age and in all its manifestations (children, young people, adults, the elderly), by promoting a culture of encounter[10] and educating with respect to the true meaning of love.

b) The Power of Love

Speaking of the "force" or "energy" of love, Cardinal Bergoglio referred directly to the Christian meaning of *agápē*, gratuitous love as a gift of self to another. It is the power of crucified love, of Christ who, once raised up from Earth, draws all to His heart by giving Himself. *Agápē* holds within itself the power of *éros* and the dynamic and generous energy of *philía*, without which love itself—

---

[9] In fact, when Cardinal Bergoglio defined the person, even though he knew that there are many ways to do so (philosophical, cultural, scientific), he preferred a theological, incarnational approach (Christ reveals the fullness of the person's humanity and dignity). That approach guides us toward the divine pedagogy through which we know *what* we are in order to learn how to *be* what we are in God's plan. In that sense, education is a real process of humanization that can be described as "knowing what humanity means" in order to be able to "learn to be what we are."

[10] In this regard, see Chapter Four below.

and also the family—would seem empty, impoverished, bloodless, lacking historicity, concreteness and a future, leaving no traces in time from which to be remembered.[11]

"Love" as Cardinal Bergoglio understood it, does not mean concentrating on oneself, or looking into one's own eyes and sighing. Rather it means taking the other by the hand and walking together toward the same goal. It means repeating to each other, "You will not die, because I will give my life for you." In that sense, family love, and the love of husband and wife, says that the only possible love is love without end, full, definitive, never in doubt, never only temporary;[12] and furthermore, it says that the trials,

---

[11] Benedict XVI, Encyclical Letter *Evangelium Vitae* (cited in this volume as "EV"), December 25, 2005, nn. 3-8; EV 23, 1543-1554.

[12] Pope Francis spoke of this aspect in his meeting with young people in Assisi on October 4, 2013, answering their questions as they met with him in the Square in front of the Basilica of Santa Maria degli Angeli "Let us think about our parents, about our grandparents and great-grandparents: They married in much poorer conditions than our own. Some married during wartime or just after a war. Some like my own parents emigrated. Where did they find the strength? They found it in the certainty that the Lord was with them, that their families were blessed by God through the Sacrament of Holy Matrimony, and that the mission of bringing children into the world and educating them is also blessed. With this assurance they overcame even the most difficult trials. These were simple certainties, but they were real; they were the pillars that supported their love. Their lives were not easy; there were problems, many, many problems. However, these simple assurances helped them to go forward. And they succeeded in having beautiful families, and in giving life and in raising their children. Dear friends, this moral and spiritual foundation is necessary in order to build well in a lasting way! Today, this foundation is no longer guaranteed by family life and the social tradition. Indeed, the society in which you were raised supports individual rights rather than the family—oh, these individual rights! It is a society that favors relationships which last until difficulties arise, and this is why it sometimes speaks about relationships between couples, within families and between spouses in a superficial and misleading way. It is enough to watch certain television

sacrifices and crises of love are no more than a necessary part of growth in goodness and truth, with no regrets and no ingratitude. A person who loves gives himself or herself completely and is never sorry for doing so, never reproachful, never counting the sacrifices made. A person who loves learns to deal with his or her own crises before the Lord, and within the family. Love is thus confirmed as a "departure with no turning back," "something never to be sorry for." Gratitude for love prevails over the fear of giving oneself to another and sacrificing for him or her. Whoever loves truly—parents, grandparents, young people, and Jesus Christ Himself—never casts something up to the other, never asks for anything back, never says, "I gave up" this or that, but instead says, like the lucky man in the Gospel, "I have found a treasure!"[13]

It is in recognizing these two "energies," "powers," that the family can be seen as the first school of the faith and of growth in humanity. In fact, as Pope Francis has said in some of his recent statements, it is in the family that we learn to love, and it is in the family that we receive the gift of faith.[14] In this context, the family

---

programs to see these values on display! How many times parish priests—sometimes I myself heard it—have this conversation with an engaged couple: "Of course you both know that marriage is for life?" "Ah, we love each other so much, but … we'll stay together as long as the love lasts. When it ends, we'll each go our separate ways." This is selfishness: When I feel like it, I'll end the marriage and forget about the "one flesh" that cannot be separated. It is risky to get married; it is risky! Selfishness is a threat; it does not know how to open up to others. Add to this the "culture of the temporary." It seems as if nothing is definitive; everything is temporary. As I said before: love, but only as long as it lasts. I once heard a seminarian—a good person—say: "I want to become a priest, but only for ten years. Then I'll rethink it." This is the culture of the temporary! But with Jesus, salvation is not *temporary*—it's *eternal!*

[13] Mt. 13:44-46

[14] For example, in his homily delivered on July 24, 2013, during Mass at the Shrine of Aparecida in Brazil, the Holy Father said, "In the face of those moments of

becomes an evangelizer because it is a human space that protects and produces life and is a first cell in which love is transmitted and in which we learn to love.

2. Two Constants: "Family and Life"

"Family and Life" became the two constants in the teaching of Cardinal Bergoglio. I would like to discuss several interrelated and fundamental points (or features) of that teaching, knowing that for Pope Francis any reflection about the family and about life itself cannot fail to take Church tradition into account. Particularly important is the Second Vatican Council, especially the Constitution *Gaudium et Spes*, as well as a careful biblical consideration of the creation of the human person "in the image and likeness of God."[15] Similarly important is a consideration of the crisis that the family is experiencing in our times,[16] balanced against the idea of the Church as the People of God ("family of families") incarnate in history. It is in that sense that the family can be defined as a Domestic Church. It lives the Gospel and faith in Jesus Christ in a particular urban

---

discouragement we experience in life, when we try to spread the Good News or to live our faith as parents in a family, I want to tell you clearly: Always know in your heart that God is by your side; He never abandons you! Let us never lose hope! Let us never extinguish it in our hearts!"

[15] In this area, Cardinal Bergoglio tracked the teaching of St. John Paul II in the Post-Synodal Apostolic Exhortation *Familiaris Consortio* of November 22, 1981 (cited in this volume as "FC"), and he made reference to the *Aparecida Document* as well.

[16] Faced with a culture of nihilism, we must create a culture of encounter. For the then-Archbishop of Buenos Aires, that meant following an incarnate realism and making the human person the center of our mission. We have to look at "flesh and blood" people in the concrete realities of their culture and their histories. See Chapter Six below.

space[17] or in those environments where it is difficult to witness one's faith or to become an evangelizer or active believer.

3. The Efficacy of Symbol and Metaphor

Pope Francis' methodology, today as then, is purposely not systematic. Coordinate clauses prevail over subordinate, and his use of symbols is extremely evocative, revealing an intuitive approach to human reality, to the family, to the mystery of God, and to an understanding of the problems that assail the Church and affect its mission in today's world. This means, concretely, that many of his reflections and expressions—sometimes syncopated, and made parenthetical by meditative silence or metaphorical allusions—follow a logic of the "unsaid." Paradoxically, they reveal more than they say, and give much food for thought about the meaning of family, the value of life, and the challenges that await each of us if we are to be credible witnesses to Jesus Christ in a world that is completely changed but that, thank God, is not totally closed off to the Gospel. Symbols, as we know, are by their nature relational and participative. Metaphors likewise open the intelligence to new meanings and to deeper reflection that would not be possible if our thoughts remained tied up in the straitjacket of definitions and stuck in the narrow passageways of concepts.

In his reflections on the family, Cardinal Bergoglio's language takes on tender notes, often delving into existential questions like "Who are we?" "Where are we going?" "Why are we here?" which strike a chord in everyone, believers and nonbelievers alike, and

---

[17] In this context, Pope Francis, in his homily at the July 27, 2013 Rio de Janeiro Mass with Bishops, priests, religious and seminarians during the 28th World Youth Day, spoke of "mission" and of being called to preach the Gospel. "God asks us to be missionaries," he said. "But where?—where He Himself places us, in our own countries or wherever He has chosen for us."

call for a clear answer. Depending on the answer, one is either in favor of life and of the process of humanization of the world and of society, or else is in favor of moving toward the death of what is human and of the deepest dimension of existence. Faith, the Cardinal emphasizes, humanizes us, just as love makes us grow up.

The Cardinal's open and direct way of speaking—which continues much in evidence in his Papacy—about the great themes of justice, love, truth, the family, the future of peoples and the mission of the Church in the world, reflects that Gospel wisdom that is found in hearts that are pure and humble. His words vibrate with the power of the *kerygma*—the proclamation—that lets them see and believe that the Church is alive, open to the will of God and able to read the signs of the times in history. This is the precious gift He offers us as we consider the family (a gift and a duty) and the great mystery of life. Moved by his many encouragements and intuitions, we see new possibilities for reflection on the vocation and rights of humankind and on the destiny of peoples; likewise[18] on freedom of conscience and on the fact that none of us can substitute our own choices for those of another, not even in ethical or biomedical matters.

All we can do is enlighten consciences and orient the men and women of our time toward truth and toward the values of life according to the demanding logic of the Gospel. We cannot under any circumstances take the place of persons and families, who must themselves decide what to do and how to act. This is true because reflection on the family and on the great mystery of life can only

---

[18] Sufficient importance should be given to the sociological analysis and the criticism of the economic model still operative in Latin America that Cardinal Bergoglio offered in the *Inaugural Conference* at the seminar *Social Debt* on September 30, 2009. See Chapter Nine below.

occur "in context,"[19] that is, taking into account the specific cultural, social, historical, political, economic and spiritual conditions of a people.

Alert to a certain methodology of leading Latin American theologians, Cardinal Bergoglio was careful about history and about the social, economic and political processes that threaten the primacy of the family, the rights of children and the fundamental freedoms of every person. His telling criticisms of poverty, of exploitation, of today's throwaway culture, of ethical relativism and of postmodern[20] ideology reveal his love for life and his conviction that "the family is the natural center of human life, which is not 'individual'; it is personal/social," and that "any opposition between person and society is a false opposition."[21]

4. The Natural Center of Human Life[22]

If it is true that loving and being loved is the answer to humankind's deepest questions and the key to the meaning of life

---

[19]   Often the sociocultural and political/economic "context" to which Cardinal Bergoglio referred is that of Latin America, where many persons are exploited or otherwise excluded from full participation in the life of the community, or that of the developed West already in decline with respect to the dignity of the human person and the value of life and of religious freedom. See, for example, the *Aparecida Document*, where it is stated, with respect to pastoral care of the family, that "the family is going through a profound crisis and the solutions offered by the Church's family, marital, and marriage preparation programs are deficient. The sacramental aspect of marriage has lost much of its value in society at large."

[20]   For discussions of the term "postmodern" and various related terms, see http://faculty.georgetown.edu/irvinem/theory/pomo.html (Trans. note)

[21]   See Chapter Four below, p. 66.

[22]   Quotations in this Section 4 that are not otherwise footnoted are taken from Chapter Four, "Parish and Family", below. (Trans. note)

itself, then in Cardinal Bergoglio's vision the family is the place where one learns to love, the natural center of human life. There being no opposition between person and society, the Cardinal looked long and hard, in his homilies, conferences and talks, at the two dimensions of the human person: individual and social. These two dimensions are not in conflict, but conflicts can exist between individual and social interests. "For this reason," the Cardinal wrote, "the Church meditates on the family, the foundation of personal and social life, and promotes it in its deepest values, defending it when it is attacked or denigrated."

a) Two essential values: stability and fruitfulness

The family, founded on Holy Matrimony, possesses two *"values that are essential in every society and every culture: stability and fruitfulness. Many in modern society tend to focus on and defend the rights of the individual, and that is a very good thing. But not for this reason can we forget the fundamental values in every society, Christian or not, that exist only in the families that are grounded in marriage. Being a father, a mother, a child, a brother or sister, a husband or wife, is at the basis of every society and without them all societies gradually lose substance and become anarchy."* This passage recalls the Concluding Report[23] of the Third General Conference of the Latin American Episcopate, Puebla, Mexico, February, 1979,[24] which itself was inspired by *Gaudium et Spes*,[25] and re-presents the four relationships described in the passage just quoted as elements that are at the base of the life of

---

[23] Referred to as the "*Puebla Document*" in this volume and cited in footnotes as "PD."

[24] Referred to in this volume as the "Puebla Conference."

[25] GS 49-50, referring to conjugal love and to the fruitfulness of Holy Matrimony.

the Church: the experience of God as father, the experience of Christ as a brother, the experience of children "in, with and for the Son," and the experience of Christ as the bridegroom of the Church. Thus, "family life reproduces these four fundamental experiences and participates in them on a smaller scale. They are four faces of human love." The Puebla Conference considered the family as the center in which these four fundamental personal relations find their fullest development. For Cardinal Bergoglio, the profound theological reason for "being a family" has its roots in the fact that the family is the image of a God who in His most profound mystery is not solitude but family. For this reason, "the law of conjugal love is communion and participation, not domination."[26]

The revelation of the one and triune God, proclaimed by Jesus Christ, *"finds its best witnesses in families from all over the world. Why? Because the family is the stable and fruitful environment of free gift and love in which the Word can be welcomed and meditated on little by little and grow like a seed that becomes a great tree. Why? Because the roles that interact in the family and that are essential for personal and social life, are also essential for God: Family life allows us to receive in an understandable way the revelation that God's love is familial. We take in the faith like mother's milk. It was not for nothing that the path by which the Lord Himself chose to reveal Himself and save us was to 'pitch His tent' in human history in that first Church, that center of communion and participation—the Holy Family of Nazareth."*

Following the Puebla Conference, Cardinal Bergoglio spoke of the strong sense of family that the peoples of Latin America and the Caribbean have, affirming that the parish—"a community of

---

[26] The expression is St. John Paul II's. He delivered the homily at the Puebla Conference during the Eucharistic Celebration.

communities and movements"—is chiefly the "family of God," a fraternity animated by a spirit of unity, not an organization chart or a territory, and still less a building. The parish is the mirror of the family, and it gathers the worries, the expectations, the hopes, the joys and the sorrows of the families that make it up. In this way, just as families don't exist in the abstract, neither can there be ideal parishes, conceived of only in the mind. If the parish really is a special place of communion and participation, it is because it reflects the dynamics of a family that is animated by faith in Jesus Christ.

In reply to the question why the family and the parish are so central, the Archbishop responded that the role of the family and of the parish is concrete, historic, settled. They are spaces for grace and produce an evangelized culture and an inculturated way of living the Gospel. These institutions guarantee to our peoples a place for development and service that other institutions are not able to manage. Centrality produces a culture, and our faith is one that becomes part of every culture. In addition, he said that in order to produce a solid and deep inculturation, faith enters into communion with those centers in which culture is in ferment, nourishes itself on that culture, enters into hearts and becomes an institution. Therefore, to be what they are, authentic "centers of communion and participation," the family and the parish must nourish and cultivate the constituent grace that they receive continuously from their own natures and from the Holy Spirit.

b) The family, the natural place of the Word of Love

Here Cardinal Bergoglio emphasized that the family is a space open to the Word and is created with the fundamental words of love, with that "I do" that establishes a covenant between husbands and wives forever. *"In the family, a newborn opens itself to the meaning of words thanks to the affection and smiles of its mother and father, and it finds the courage to speak. In the family, the word is identified with the person who speaks it and all have a voice: children, young people, adults and the elderly. In the family the word can be trusted because it holds the memory of affectionate gestures and it accompanies new acts of affection every day. This point can be summarized by saying that the family is the place of the word because it is centered on love. Words said and listened to in the family never disappear; they circle around the heart, illuminating it, guiding it, giving it encouragement. A father's advice, the prayer learned reading a mother's lips, a secret shared with a brother or sister, the stories told by grandparents ... these are the words that make up the little universe that every heart treasures."*

In summary, faith passes through the life of the family and nourishes itself with that irreplaceable affective dimension which no one can do without. It is the anthropological dimension of being and of belief in Jesus Christ! The family thus carries out a fundamental task of historical mediation of the gift of faith and the proclamation of the Gospel. Such mediation makes everyone responsible actors as genuine mediators. Cardinal Bergoglio emphasized that while an intermediary seeks to get for him or herself a benefit from each side, a mediator keeps nothing for him or herself but rather spends generously, even to the point of exhausting all resources, knowing that the other's good is the real gain.

The grace of love, in the family and in the parish, enables us to accept others freely and to learn to pardon. Family and parish are open spaces of love and they constitute a training ground for life where we learn how to welcome everyone, without excluding anyone. *"The family and the parish are the place of welcome, of the communion of deep love, rather than of fashions that change continuously.... Family values are valid and vital for every human heart: the centrality of the family, the protection from the outside offered by the door of one's home, the family intimacy within, the simple joy of the family dinner table, home as the place where we recover when sick and where all take their rest, where we can accept and be accepted just as we are."*

c) Challenges to the family today

In his reflections on the family, the Cardinal spoke of the crisis of social and moral values that today's families are suffering. There are challenges in the face of which the Church cannot remain helpless or appear to have no resources or concrete solutions to offer. In that sense, the widespread challenges affecting families have also become challenges to evangelization and inculturation of the Gospel.

The first challenge consists in recentering the family on Christ and in empowering the baptized person to generate a Christian culture. In other words, to becoming an evangelizer who will bring the Gospel to his or her brothers and sisters, especially the most marginalized. This is a new perspective on evangelization. The *kerygma* must focus on the whole person in his or her communitary dimension. Faced with a cultural crisis of unanticipated dimensions, Cardinal Bergoglio, harking back to paragraph 52 of St. John Paul II's 1990 Encyclical *Redemptoris Missio*, wrote that a special effort was needed to inculturate the message of Jesus in a way that enables Christian values to transform the various cores of culture, purifying them if necessary, and enabling a strengthened Christian culture that renews, extends and unifies past and present historical values to address the challenges of our time. *"The fact is that the center is a profoundly constituent element of our Latin American culture, a culture that is strongly 'circular.' It helps to keep this in mind to be able to understand many things that can't be understood if one begins from a linear, rationalistic concept that considers progress to require an abandonment of the center, as an emergence of new things that have nothing to do with the old ... Culture and faith have been created from and revolve around specific centers of 'communion and participation': spatial centers, like shrines, and temporal centers, like the great feasts, in which communion and participation reach their greatest splendor."* We have to strengthen these centers, which are necessary for the birth and life of a culture because they ensure its stability and fruitfulness.

The second challenge is essentially the struggle against a culture of exclusion and marginalization.[27] Great swaths of the world's population are excluded and marginalized by the phenomenon of globalization and by new technologies. We are not dealing simply with poverty, exploitation and oppression, but rather with something new: People who are excluded are not only exploited, they are treated as "leftovers" to be "thrown away"—the trash of a technologically advanced society. A dualistic culture has been created where what seems the most modern and progressive coexists with what is considered merely old and useless, all of which produces a breakdown of Christian tradition.

The third challenge that Cardinal Bergoglio noted is secularization, which restricts faith and the Church to private individual matters. To avoid this phenomenon we must rediscover

---

[27] On this point the Cardinal gives his greatest attention to the social context in which the family finds itself. See AD *passim.*

the public and communitary character of the Faith, relying especially on the formation of the laity and the evangelization of well-educated professionals. Formation for witness and for an understanding of the ecclesial aspect of the faith is a complex process that takes time and that involves the world of young people, where youth ministry must deal with social changes that affect the people it serves.

To answer these three great challenges, Cardinal Bergoglio saw pastoral activity, catechetical and social, as the most effective way to transmit and strengthen the faith in the community, especially among the young. Catechesis is one of the pillars of pastoral activity and a key element in the process of evangelization. Its complement, social service, enables faith to be reconnected with life, and worship to be reconnected with witness to Gospel values in our personal, family and social lives.

The fourth challenge, whose changes affect the evangelizing activities of the Church, is the economy. The continuing economic crisis that we are experiencing shows that we need to learn how to use material goods in a way that produces a more just way of life, one that shows proper concern for the least of our brothers and sisters. This challenge, according to Cardinal Bergoglio, requires us to recognize the social debt we owe to the society of which we are a part. This social debt arises from deprivations that constitute a serious risk to life, to the dignity of the person, and to opportunities for human development.[28] Social debt is also an existential debt related to a crisis in the meaning of life. To pay this social debt we must weave a social fabric and build societal bonds. This is an anthropological question because it touches the dignity of the

---

[28] See Chapter Nine below.

person and his or her place in a people. Greater poverty also affects social exclusion and contributes to a throwaway culture.

The Cardinal's criticisms were strong: *"Current culture tends to offer lifestyles that are not natural and that offend human dignity. The dominant impact of the idols of power, wealth and fleeting pleasure has enabled them, heedless of the value of the human person, to become the accepted standards of behavior and the decisive criteria for social organization. The economic and social crisis and the consequent growth of poverty are caused by policies inspired by variations of economic theory that, to the detriment of the dignity of persons and peoples, consider profit and market forces to be absolutes. ... The loss of the sense of justice and the lack of respect for others have become more pronounced and have led to a situation of inequality. The consequence of this situation is the concentration of natural, financial and informational wealth in the hands of a few, with consequent further increases in inequality and exclusion."*

Poverty is not a chance effect of progress. It is rather the foreseeable result of economic, social and political situations and structures.[29] Social debt demands the implementation of social justice and calls to account all social forces, especially government, politicians, the financial sector, business people, the food and agriculture industry, manufacturing, extractive industries, corporate leaders, unions, churches and so on. Social debt calls for an ethical commitment, inspired by Gospel values, that produces an economy of gift and sharing, the medicine that heals every form of injustice and poverty.

---

[29] See the teaching of St. John Paul II and Pope Emeritus Benedict XVI as set out in the Encyclical *Deus Caritas Est.*

5. Welcome and Care for All Ages: Children, Young People, the Elderly

Archbishop Bergoglio delivered a beautiful homily at the Mass for Life on March 25, 2011, in the Cathedral of Buenos Aires.[30] Speaking of the experience of Mary, who welcomed the words of the Archangel Gabriel and followed Jesus' life day by day—from Nazareth, to Bethlehem, to exile, to Nazareth, to Jerusalem and finally to Calvary—Cardinal Bergoglio showed how every Christian, following the example of the Blessed Mother, is called to accompany life in all its stages.

Pope Benedict XVI declared 2011 "the Year of Life." During that year Cardinal Bergoglio asked how each of us welcomes life— from the moment of conception until death. He put the question this way: *"Do we know how to accompany life? The life of our kids, of those who are our children and those who are not,.... Do we know how to encourage kids as they are growing up? Do we know where to put limits? What about the kids who are not ours, do I worry about the ones who seem to have no one? They are life too! God has breathed life into everyone! Or do I take better care of my pets? Do I take care of my babies as they grow up? Do I watch who their friends are? Do I make sure they grow up adult and free? Do I know how to teach my children freedom? Do I know how they spend their free time? Life grew and Mary continued to accompany it. And you? What do you do? Do you think about your parents and grandparents, your in-laws? Do you look out for them, worry about them? Visit them? Sometimes life becomes very difficult, sometimes they have to go into a senior-care facility because of health or problems in the family, but when they go, do you take a*

---

[30] Chapter Ten below.

Saturday or Sunday to visit them? Do you take care of cherished lives that are fading away but that gave you life?"[31]

Reading this page reminded me of a homily that Archbishop Oscar Arnulfo Romero, himself a martyr in 1980, delivered at the funeral of a priest assassinated by a death squad: *"The Second Vatican Council tells us that not everyone will have the honor of shedding blood, of dying, for the Faith, but God asks all who believe in Him to have the spirit of a martyr. All of us must be ready to die for our faith, even if the Lord does not grant us that honor. Yes, let us be ready so that when our time comes to give an account of our lives we can say, 'Lord, I was ready to give my life for You. And I did.' Giving one's life doesn't mean only being killed; giving one's life, having the spirit of a martyr, means honoring duty, in silence, in prayer, in the faithful doing of one's duty, in that silence of daily life, giving one's life little by little. Just like a mother does when with the simplicity of maternal martyrdom and without fear she conceives a child, brings it into the world, nourishes it, raises it and looks after it with love. That is what giving one's life means. That is martyrdom ...."*

In speaking of life—that of Jesus as well as ours and our parents' and that of the Church—Cardinal Bergoglio gave a name and a face to those who make up the family, to let us know that we must take care of every age of life. His methodology reflects wisdom and a biblical view of time and of the family. It is as if to say, "There is an age, a time, for everything."[32] In this passage the biblical author offers a poetic meditation on the ages of humanity, on the mystery that accompanies human life from beginning to end. All the ages of humanity pass in review, unstoppably but also

---

[31] *Ibid.*

[32] Wis. 3:1-15

monotonously and apparently predetermined. Yet a radical question of meaning surrounds them, raised by the biblical author, who asks it in the name of a restless humanity in search of meaning. It is a passage of extraordinary power, astonishingly modern, and radically committed to finding meaning. For Cardinal Bergoglio the answer was simple: To discover the meaning of life we must take care of every one of its ages, of all our days from conception until life on Earth is bid farewell.

Taking care of the ages of life means recognizing an integrated vision of the person in his or her individual and social dimension. Today, like then, Pope Francis gives significant attention to the close ties that exist between young people and the elderly, ties that are often misunderstood by society and by the hedonistic culture in which our children grow up these days. Taking care of life at every age means sowing hope and giving a future to humanity itself. *"A people who doesn't take care of its children and the elderly is a people in decline; take care of children and of the elderly because they are the future of the people: children because they are the force that will carry the country forward, and the elderly because they are the treasure of wisdom that guides that force. Force and wisdom ... taking care of life means sowing hope."*[33]

Children, young adults, parents and the elderly are the ones we think about when we think about the family and about life. In his reflection on *The Family in the Light of the Aparecida Document,*[34] Cardinal Bergoglio, speaking of the person, said, *"...the Aparecida Document deals at length*[35] *with children, adolescents and younger adults; the well-being of the elderly; the dignity and participation*

---

[33] See Chapter Thirteen below.

[34] See Chapter One below.

[35] AD 438-475

of women; the responsibility of men, as such and as fathers of families; the culture of life and protection of the environment. Each one of these 'persons' is profoundly linked to the family."

Without commenting on every condition and every challenge that these persons face, Cardinal Bergoglio examined two stages of life that he considered crucial to greater peace between generations: childhood and old age. They are the two extremes of life and are the most vulnerable and the most forgotten. "A society that abandons its babies and that ignores its elderly is endangering its own future."[36] Babies are God's blessing and a sign of His presence in the world!

Following the model of the *Aparecida Document*, Cardinal Bergoglio criticized the conditions of poverty, suffering and violence that many children and young people live in, making special reference to child labor, to homeless and abused children, and to those who are HIV-positive, to orphans, to child soldiers, to children who are exploited and embittered, the victims of pornography and of prostitution, both virtual and real. *"This situation speaks to us of an ever-deeper and more widespread moral degradation. It leads us to ask how we can rekindle respect for the lives and the dignity of our children. We are robbing many of them of their youth and are endangering both their future and ours. This is a responsibility that we share as a society and that weighs most heavily on those who have greater power, education and wealth.*

"We have to recognize that every boy or girl who is marginalized, abandoned or living on the streets, with scant access to education and healthcare, is a living example not only of injustice but also of the breakdown of institutions—the family and its

---

[36] See Chapter One below.

neighborhood network, local charities, the parish, and all the different government agencies.'[37] In this regard, the Gospel warning is clear and strong: "Who welcomes even one of these little ones in My name, welcomes Me."[38] "See that you do not mistreat one of these little ones, for I say to you that their angels in heaven always look upon the face of My heavenly Father."[39]

At the other end of life, Cardinal Bergoglio saw the elderly, who are the memory of our family, of society itself. He calls them "repositories of the collective memory of the nation and the family."[40] Following the model of the *Aparecida Document* and of the Bible, he warns that old age should be a blessing, not a curse: *"Being old, in the context of postmodern culture, means belonging to something that is no longer in style, that is worn-out, that has no voice. Many seniors are considered to have no economic value.... Senior-care and senior-living facilities sometimes become 'warehouses for the elderly.' [In contrast,] the Aparecida Document encourages intergenerational dialogue, respect for and gratitude to the elderly, recognition of their labors and human and spiritual attention to their needs.'*[41]

For Cardinal Bergoglio, the family is "the environment where the elderly are welcome and understood."[42] They are a gift for the Church, they support us with their prayers and with their wisdom, and it is through them that prophetic voices can be heard in the Church and in the world.

---

[37] *Ibid.*

[38] Mt. 18:5

[39] Mt. 18:10

[40] See Chapter One below.

[41] AD 447-450

[42] *Ibid.*

Human and spiritual attention to the elderly is a real challenge for ecclesial communities today. It is a challenge that Pope Francis launches when he speaks of a throwaway culture and of the ever-greater divergence between the world of the young and the world of the elderly.

In that context, it is worthwhile to quote from the talk that Pope Francis gave to young people in the Cathedral of St. Sebastian on July 25, 2013 during the Rio de Janeiro World Youth Day:

"At this moment, I think our world civilization has gone beyond its limits; it has gone beyond its limits because it has made money into such a god that we are now faced with a philosophy and a practice which exclude the two ends of life that are most full of promise for peoples. Exclusion of the elderly, obviously. We might think that there exists a kind of hidden euthanasia in that we don't take care of the elderly; but there is also a cultural euthanasia, since we don't allow them to speak, we don't allow them to act. And there is the exclusion of the young. The percentage of our young people without work, without employment, is very high, and we have a generation with no experience of the dignity gained through work. This civilization, in other words, has led us to exclude the two peaks that make up our future. As for the young, they must emerge, they must assert themselves; the young must go out to fight for values, to fight for these values; and the elderly must open their mouths, the elderly must open their mouths and teach us! Pass on to us the wisdom of the peoples!

"Here with my fellow Argentinians, I implore the elderly, from my heart: Do not cease to be the cultural treasury of our people, a treasury that hands on justice, hands on history, hands on values, hands on the memory of the people. And the rest of you, please, do not oppose the elderly: Let them speak, listen to them and go forward. But know this, know that at this moment, you young

people and you elderly people are condemned to the same destiny: exclusion. Don't allow yourselves to be excluded. It's obvious! That's why I think you must work. Faith in Jesus Christ is not a joke. It is something very serious. It is a scandal that God came to be one of us. It is a scandal that He died on a cross. It is a scandal: the scandal of the Cross. The Cross continues to provoke scandal. But it is the one sure path, the path of the Cross, the path of Jesus, the path of the Incarnation of Jesus. Please do not water down your faith in Jesus Christ. We dilute fruit drinks—orange, apple, banana juice—but please do not drink a diluted form of faith. Faith is whole and entire, not something you water down. It is faith in Jesus. It is faith in the Son of God made man, who loved me and who died for me. So make yourselves heard! Take care of the two ends of the population: the elderly and the young. Do not allow yourselves to be excluded. Do not allow the elderly to be excluded."

During the mid-day Angelus of July 26, 2013, standing on the balcony of the Archbishop's residence in Rio de Janeiro, Pope Francis quoted from the *Aparecida Document* as follows: *"Children and the elderly are the future of peoples; children because they carry history forward, and the elderly because they pass on the experience and wisdom of their lives."*[43] This relationship, this dialogue between generations, is a treasure to guard and an investment to grow. That day was also the Feast of Saints Joachim and Anna; celebrating them the Pope said: *"Saints Joachim and Anna are at the end of a long line that, in the warmth of the family, passed on faith and the love of God to Mary, who welcomed the Son of God in her womb and gave Him to the world, to us. Great is the*

---

[43] AD 447

value of the family as the special place for the transmission of the Faith!

"With respect to the family I would like to emphasize one more thing: Today, on the feast of Saints Joachim and Anna, Grandparents Day is celebrated in Brazil and in many other countries. How important they are in the life of the family as they communicate that heritage of humanity and faith that is essential in every society! And how important is the encounter and dialogue between generations, especially within the family!"

When the two poles of life are no longer held together, both the family and society risk breakdown. The Church's task is to work to keep these two poles closely bound through a culture of welcome and encounter.

The Bible has high praise for the beauty and strength of youth, and in the youth the elderly find support and warmth. The ornament of youth is above all strength,[44] that of the elderly is wisdom[45]. On the other hand, indecision and timidity,[46] as well as rejection of certain tasks,[47] based on awareness of lack of experience,[48] are typical of youth; and growing weakness is characteristic of the elderly. A person who is growing old fears being marginalized and left alone. Still, however, in ancient Israel the elderly were the ones who had the right to address the community and to act as judges. The person who has grown old is the one who proclaims to new generations the power and justice of God that was taught to that person from his or her youth by God

---

[44] Pv. 20:29

[45] Jb. 12:12

[46] Jgs. 8:20

[47] Jer. 1:6

[48] 1 Kg. 3:7 et seq.; 1 Sam. 17:33

Himself.[49] Without the elderly, there is no more memory and thus no future, because memory always looks to the future; by treasuring the past, it clarifies the present and paves the way for a history beyond today. Without young people, we are doomed to death and to a life without hope, unsuccessful, incapable of performing acts of great renewal and profound change.

These two poles of life, youth and old age, offer a harmonious vision of time that in the Bible is structured differently from what we imagine and that is never reduced to the simple duration of a phenomenon. Time is always a *kairós*, a favorable time, good and opportune for encountering God and experiencing salvation.

6. The Icon of the Presentation of Jesus in the Temple

The Holy Family of Nazareth is traditionally presented as the truest and most concrete example of the family, of how families should be, of a "Domestic Church"[50] in which the family seeks to live out the Gospel of love. Still, beside this very early image of the family there is another that shows more clearly that every family is linked to the generations that precede it and that it can have a future only if it treasures the forward-looking memory represented, as Cardinal Bergoglio said, by the union of the two poles of life: youth and old age.

This other image comes to us from the Gospel of Luke, which describes the Presentation of Jesus in the Temple.[51] The artist Giotto portrays this scene dramatically in the right transept of the Lower Basilica of Assisi: the elderly Simeon, representing prophecy inspired by the Holy Spirit, holds Jesus. Anna the

---

[49] Ps. 71:9, 17-19, 20

[50] FC 49

[51] Lk. 2:22-38

33

prophetess, along in years, is portrayed praising God and announcing salvation for those who were awaiting the redemption of Israel. In Luke's narrative, as Joseph and Mary enter the Temple with their baby Jesus to fulfill the precepts of the Law, Simeon—who represented the forward-looking memory of Israel—is moved by the Spirit and recognizes in that baby the Light unto the Nations.[52] Likewise, the prophetess Anna, long close to the Lord and custodian of the expectations of her People, carries in her heart the blessing of God and the certainty that every hope can be realized in that baby. These two elders announce to future generations the power and justice of God, who has redeemed us in an infant, and they are passers-on of that promise that finds its origin in the Bosom of Abraham. They are "embers that hold, like coals hold fire, the values that make us great,"[53] and they say to us that every family, like the Holy Family of Nazareth, has a place in the history of a people but could not exist without the generations that came before it.

In the meeting between aged Simeon and a young mother, Mary, Old and New Testament (two "generations") unite in a wondrous fashion and in thanksgiving for the gift of the Light that shone in the darkness and kept the darkness from prevailing. The Holy Family of Nazareth, a Domestic Church, becomes, in the light of the Presentation, a "family of families" heir to a promise that at

---

[52] Simeon addresses the God of the Covenant directly—the God for whom the Temple was built—and he speaks of the fulfillment of what he had been waiting for all his life, what the whole People of the Old Testament was waiting for. He speaks of the Light that "illuminates the Gentiles" [pagans] (Lk. 2:32), of the Light that is the glory of the People of God. The Light is the crowning of their expectations and hopes, of the opening of the Temple to the God of the Covenant through sacrifice.

[53] Chapter Six below.

last has been fulfilled, because the Father, in Christ, by the power of the Holy Spirit, has cared for all the family of Abraham.[54]

---

[54] Heb. 2:16

CHAPTER ONE

THE FAMILY IN THE LIGHT OF THE APARECIDA DOCUMENT[55]

"There is no doubt that the enthusiastic proclamation of the Gospel of the family and life as 'marvelous news,' and a deepening of the identity and mission of the domestic Church, the sanctuary of life, as a truth that fully humanizes husbands and wives, children and humanity, has a special place in the heart of our Universal Pastor."

With these words, Cardinal Alfonso López Trujillo began his lecture on *The Family in the Pontificate of John Paul II* at the October 18, 2003 Symposium celebrating the Twenty-Fifth Anniversary of the Pontificate of St. John Paul II.[56] I think these words—spoken by one who was not only President of the Pontifical Council for the Family but also a loyal and tireless worker for the last two Popes[57]—are the perfect summary of the teaching of St. John Paul II, who saw Holy Matrimony and the family as both a *gift* and a *commitment.*

We mourn the loss of the Cardinal, but we are grateful to God for his life and ministry, for his selflessness and for his warmth and friendship. I had the pleasure of working closely with him during the Aparecida Conference. To be precise, it is in the context of this, my last meeting with His Eminence, that I would like to reflect on

---

[55] Originally published in the Spanish edition of *Familia et Vita* (XIII, 2/3 2008, pp. 63-71).

[56] See the following URL:
http://www.vatican.va/roman_curia/pontifical_councils/family/documents/ rc_pc_family_doc_20031018_riflessioni-trujillo_en.html

[57] St. John Paul II and Pope Emeritus Benedict XVI (Trans. note)

what was discussed then and was afterward reflected in the *Aparecida Document*. A large part of what is said in that document about the family were his ideas and suggestions, so I want us to remember him and his wisdom as I comment on the different aspects of the document,

I have said in the past that the *Aparecida Document* reflects what we bishops lived out in the assembly hall, but it also expresses the feeling of the faithful people of God who accompanied us with their prayers and celebrations from *above*, that is, from the Aparecida Shrine Church itself. We were downstairs in the Shrine's meeting hall, and above—in the church—thousands and thousands of pilgrims prayed for our work. This context has remained, in a way, an integral part of the document, and it reflects a fundamental principle for the whole Church of Latin America and the Caribbean: We become "disciples and missionaries of Jesus Christ—Way, Truth and Life—so that we may have abundant life in Him."[58] The mission of the Church cannot be fruitful if we do not allow ourselves to be invited by the Lord to follow Him more closely. The disciple is also a missionary by reason of his encounter with the Lord who is living and active in our lives. It is precisely this principle that becomes the paradigm for our evangelizing action.

The Family, Patrimony of Humanity and Treasure of Our Peoples

The *Aparecida Document* presents the history of the Church in Latin America and the Caribbean, as well as the challenges of the

---

[58] Jn. 10:10

previous conferences of CELAM. In this sense, the family is of key importance and continues to be a priority in the new evangelization. The *Puebla Document* had already said this clearly: "The family is one of the centers of communion and participation and has a direct influence in the journey of the majority of the peoples of our continent."[59] The *Aparecida Document* presents the family as the "patrimony of humanity,"[60] a phrase of our Supreme Pontiff that expresses the natural, and at the same time theological, foundation of Holy Matrimony and of the family.

The first reflection on the family in the *Aparecida Document* is found in its Chapter Six, where the document speaks of the *places* where missionary disciples are formed. That chapter says that the family is not only the "patrimony of humanity" but also the "most valuable treasure of our Latin American people."[61] This treasure is a rich vein that has not yet been fully mined. If it is true that the family has suffered considerable erosion in our postmodern society, we still have confidence in the richness that it represents. The family is precisely one of the few *places* in our social fabric that continues to be a value and goal that most people want to reach: living in a family, having a family. In a society where everything has a "price," this "treasure" is a free gift that is attained only through love and mutual giving. The *Aparecida Document* presents the family as the "first school of faith." The family itself has and is the "place and the school of communion, the source of human and civic values, and the home where human life is born and is welcomed generously and responsibly."[62]

---

[59] PD 568-569

[60] AD 302, 432

[61] AD 302

[62] AD 302

When it says "place and school of communion," the *Aparecida Document* summarizes what was said in the *Puebla Document* and is expressed in abundance in the teaching of St. John Paul II. In order for a family community to exist, its members must take the risk of living in communion. It is there that new generations learn to be "people of communion." In this way, the family is a "font" for all those values that society so urgently needs, values that have self-giving as their fundamental principle. Family solidarity is the source of civic values, which have their concrete expression in mutual respect and civil harmony. All this we learn in the bosom of our families. These values appear spontaneously, but not without struggle and discernment, in a multitude of family situations. When we say "home," we consider something much more valuable than square footage in a "house": "home" is a nest, a cradle of life. It is the privileged setting of life received with responsibility, educated with generous giving, celebrated with festive joy, fed with the bread of work and of tears, healed when it is injured, and mourned when it is gone. Our nations are true homes, where tenderness and firmness join hands in the continuing education of our children.

The family is likewise a "school of faith." Faith presupposes nature, and it is from the communion of these two dimensions that the missionary disciple answers his or her call. Nature receives faith in the family and, if it is a believing family, God entrusts the mother and father with the gift of faith. When they take their children to be baptized, the Church tells them, "You are a Domestic Church." Since parents are the first educators in the faith, they need all the support the Church can give them to carry out this mission. Family pastoral ministry is thus a priority for each diocese. The family, together with the parish, then becomes the "first place for the Christian initiation of children," offering them a "Christian idea of existence and assisting them in the formulation of their plan for life as missionary disciples."[63]

Family, Persons and Life

The third part of the document speaks to our peoples about the life of Jesus Christ. That is where—in Chapter Nine—the theme of "the family" is reintroduced. The Conference felt it appropriate to deal with questions of Holy Matrimony and the family, but to leave to the individual Episcopal Conferences the ability to address those questions more fully.[64] The larger context in which these points are developed is that of life understood as a gift and as a commitment to be kept and strengthened.

The document repeats what it had earlier said about the family as a "patrimony and a treasure." It lists the difficult life situations that many families encounter, and that threaten the family as an institution. Some of those situations are poverty and economic hardship; migration to find work or to escape the violence that pervades many parts of our continent and destroys family ties; the increase in sexual abuse within families; divorce, which has become a right, but which causes irreparable damage to the spirit and personalities of the children; the anti-life campaigns, which, with the support of the media and lawmakers, are gaining ground among our peoples, and are targeting life at its most defenseless—the unborn and the abandoned elderly. Though the document deals with these questions in terms of individuals, its framework reflects an inclusive and firm reliance on God's larger plan for Holy Matrimony and the family, and it calls on us as missionary disciples

---

[63] *Ibid.*
[64] AD 431

to "work to change this situation, and help the family assume its identity and its mission in society and in the Church."[65]

Accordingly, in the sections that follow, the document deals with the doctrinal foundations of Holy Matrimony and the family. Made sacred by the Sacrament of Holy Matrimony, the family is a sign of God's love for humanity and of the commitment of Christ to his Church, a covenant that manifests itself in the complex of family relationships and in the building of a better world.[66] It repeats the very beautiful image of the family as an icon of the Trinity, which was so emphasized by both St. John Paul II and Cardinal López Trujillo.[67] Given the importance of the family, its strengthening and development are especially important for evangelization. In every diocese there should be an "intense and vigorous" family ministry that proclaims the gospel of the family, promotes the culture of life, and works to ensure that the rights of the family are recognized and respected.[68] The *Aparecida Document* asks that government officials, lawmakers, and healthcare professionals defend the value of life and support conscientious objection to government regulations that are unjust in the light of faith and reason. The document then deals with "Eucharistic Consistency," that is: "realizing that one cannot receive Holy Communion and at the same time violate the Commandments in word or deed, particularly words or deeds that support abortion, euthanasia and other serious crimes against life and the family. This responsibility weighs especially on lawmakers, government officials and healthcare professionals."[69] On this point, I remember in particular

---

[65] AD 432
[66] AD 433
[67] AD 434
[68] AD 435
[69] AD 436

the speech of Cardinal López Trujillo during the Eleventh Ordinary General Assembly of the Synod of Bishops,[70] where he used the words I just quoted and urged Christians, especially politicians and lawmakers, to live out this "Eucharistic Consistency."

Preparation for the Sacrament of Holy Matrimony

Among the guidelines that the *Aparecida Document* proposes for family pastoral ministry, I would like to discuss the following one in particular: "Renewal of the remote and proximate preparation for the Sacrament of Holy Matrimony and family life using faith-oriented educational materials."[71] This proposal is taken from the document *Preparation for the Sacrament of Holy Matrimony* issued by the Pontifical Council for the Family on May 13, 1996. The theme was first examined by St. John Paul II in that "Magna Carta" for the family: *Familiaris Consortio.*[72] I think this challenge is fundamental for the Church on our continent. We see a noticeable drop in Church marriages. Young people today prefer simply to live together and not take on a lifelong commitment. Economic instability and housing shortages in our large cities force less- well-off couples to live with their parents. On the other hand, we see the same thing in wealthier areas, where young people opt for a "trial marriage" and put off having children until they feel comfortable and settled.   In fact, the whole notion of Holy Matrimony is falling apart, and it is time to proclaim the Good News of Holy Matrimony and the Family. So far, so good, but to do this we have to reexamine the methodology of so-called "marriage prep courses." In many cases these are no more than a Pastor's chat

---

[70] Delivered on October 7, 2005

[71] AD 437c

[72] FC , n. 66

with a group of engaged couples. I believe we need to update the content and form of these courses, using simple but substantive language clearly explaining how, for baptized persons, marriage is a Sacrament. The *Aparecida Document* lists the essential elements of a preparation course: an opportunity for engaged couples to grow in human and religious maturity, become aware of the nature and purposes of marriage, and celebrate and live it as a Sacrament that becomes a true *kairós* for them. Even if in many dioceses there has been progress in this regard, the different stages of preparation are such that much still remains to be done. Traditional piety offers hope that our communities will reawaken to this process, given the strong values and regular practices that our Latin American and Caribbean families maintain. If the family is a value, so should Holy Matrimony be as well, since it is the foundation of the family.

Persons

In the second part of Chapter Nine, the *Aparecida Document* deals at length with children, adolescents and young people; with the well-being of the elderly; with the dignity and participation of women; with the responsibility of men, as such and as fathers of families; with the culture of life, and with protection of the environment.[73] Each one of these "persons" is profoundly linked to the family. Life and ecology are the first responsibility of the family, but they are also a responsibility of society as a whole.

Without commenting extensively on every challenge faced by these persons, I want to focus particularly on two stages of life, namely childhood and old age, that I consider fundamental for an increase of peace among the several generations. They are the two

---

[73] AD 438-475

endpoints of life, and, on our continent, they are the most vulnerable and the most neglected. A society that abandons its children and warehouses its seniors is a society that is putting its own future in jeopardy. I wrote a letter about children and adolescents at risk on the occasion of the Thirty-First Youth Pilgrimage to the Shrine of Our Lady of Luján.[74] In that letter I described a situation that is similar to what is described in the *Aparecida Document*. What our children and adolescents have to suffer in many of our large cities on this continent is a sin. This hard reality hurts and shocks us, but it opens our hearts and should drive us to take direct action to save these children, the Lord's dearest treasure.

The *Aparecida Document* describes the dramatic situation of many children this way: *"It is painful to see the poverty, domestic violence—especially in homes that are broken or where the parents are not married—and sexual abuse that affect a great number of our children: children working illegally, street children, children with HIV/AIDS, orphans, child soldiers, boys and girls deceived with promises of work and exposed to pornography and forced into prostitution, both virtual and real. Early childhood (from birth to six years) is especially in need of attention and care. We cannot remain indifferent to the suffering of so many innocent children."*[75]

This reality speaks to us of an ever-deeper and more widespread moral degradation. It leads us to ask how we can rekindle respect for the lives and the dignity of our children. We are robbing many of them of their youth and are endangering both their future and ours. This is a responsibility that we share as a

---

[74] See Chapter Seven below.
[75] AD 439

society and that weighs most heavily on those who have greater power, education and wealth.

We have to recognize that every boy or girl who is marginalized, abandoned or living on the streets, with scant access to education and healthcare, is a living example not only of injustice but also of the breakdown of institutions—the family and its neighborhood network, local charities, the parish, and all the different government agencies. Many of these situations call for an immediate response, but not with a lot of fanfare. The search for, and practical application of, solutions should not be a patchwork exercise. We need a change of heart and mind that leads us to value these children and give them a life worth living, from their mother's womb until they rest in the arms of God their Father, and we must put that approach into practice every day.

We must enter into the heart of God and begin to listen to the voices of the weakest among us—these children and adolescents—and remember the words of the Lord: "Whoever receives one child such as this in My name receives Me."[76] and "See that you do not mistreat one of these little ones, for I say to you that their angels in heaven always look upon the face of My heavenly Father."[77]

At the other extreme of life are the elderly. They are repositories of the collective memory of the nation and the family. The *Aparecida Document* describes old age as a good, not as a misfortune. On the other hand, being elderly in the cultural context of postmodernity means being out of date, "over the hill," without anything to say. According to some economic theories, many seniors are simply financial burdens by reason of their increasing life expectancies and their healthcare needs. In some families

---

[76] Mt. 18:5

[77] Mt 18:10

grandparents and older family members are excluded. Some institutions and senior-care facilities have become nothing more than warehouses for the elderly. This situation is treated in the *Aparecida Document*, and its basic message is that the elderly must be a welcome part of the family, Church and society. The *Aparecida Document* encourages an intergenerational dialogue, respect and gratitude for our elders, recognition of their hard work, and attention to their human and spiritual needs.[78]

The family is the place where the elderly are welcome and supported. The Church as well celebrates the gift that the elderly are in many parish communities. Today they are our principal and most numerous worshipers at liturgical celebrations. They devote a good portion of their time to the poor, they visit hospitals and senior living facilities, and they are missionaries in vast areas of our continent. Their prayer sustains the Church. The counsel of our elders has saved more than one priestly and religious vocation. Lastly, with their physical and spiritual sufferings, they give us an example of strength and apostolic zeal. An example of all of this has been the witness of our dear St. John Paul II. But if the elderly have a place in our Church, it is not that way in secular society as a whole, and it is important to support caring and fair policies that make our elderly full members of society and not simply recipients of politically-motivated handouts. What's needed is a community where all are welcome, rather than isolated facilities where the elderly can live without "bothering" us.

Human and spiritual care for the elderly is a true challenge for our ecclesial communities. The elderly are "disciples and missionaries" with a specific vocation: that of giving common

---

[78] AD 447-450

sense and maturity to the younger generations and of being teachers of prayer and of generous commitment.

Culture of Life and Concern for the Environment

Chapter Nine of the *Aparecida Document* concludes with a strong defense of the culture of life[79] and concern for the environment.[80] Both realities are united by respect for God's plan for creation. Without God there is no respect for life. Life stops being a person with a right and becomes a commodity. Our peoples still respect life, but they are influenced by the culture of death. *"The desire for life, peace, fraternity, and happiness finds no fulfillment amid the idols of profit and efficiency, insensitivity to the suffering of others, attacks on life in the womb, infant mortality, disrepair and neglect in some hospitals, and violence against children and youth, men and women. All this underscores the importance of fighting for life, and for the dignity and integrity of the human person. The strongest defense of that dignity and of these values begins in the family."*[81]

With regard to concern for the environment, we are squandering the rich natural resources of our continent. *"Today the natural wealth of Latin America and the Caribbean is being subjected to foolish exploitation that everywhere in our region is leaving ruin and even death in its wake. A great deal of the responsibility for this entire process must be placed on an economic model that in practice values the excessive pursuit of wealth over the lives of individuals and peoples, and over a*

---

[79] AD 464-469

[80] AD 470-475

[81] AD 468

reasonable respect for nature. The devastation of our forests and biodiversity that is the fruit of selfish and predatory policies gives rise to moral responsibility on the part of those who engage in it, because it embitters the lives of millions of persons, especially the rural populations and indigenous peoples, who are driven out into nonproductive land or into the large cities where they live in overcrowded slums. Our region needs to direct its agro-industrial activities toward the development of the richness of its land and of human resources in the service of the common good, and we can't fail to point out the problems that are caused by the thoughtless and unregulated industrialization of our cities and countryside that pollutes the environment with all sorts of organic and chemical wastes. The same alarm must be raised with respect to extractive industries, which, if they do not adopt procedures for limiting and offsetting the negative effects they have on the environment, will destroy our forests, pollute our water, and end up turning the land into an endless desert.[82]

Faced with this situation, it is urgent that we *"evangelize our peoples to discover the gift of creation, so that they learn how to contemplate and care for it as the home of all living creatures and the source of the planet's life. In that way they will exercise responsible human stewardship over the Earth and its resources, making those resources fruitful for all, and they will be led to live lives of reserved and modest solidarity."*[83] The first place for this awareness is likewise the family, which must be evangelized to an appreciation of God's plan for all creation.

We see that the reality of our continent and of the Caribbean presents significant challenges to an evangelization that includes

---

[82] AD 473
[83] AD 474a

human development as well as the proclamation of salvation in Christ.

In conclusion, and relying on the intercession of Our Lady and St. Joseph, let us make our own the prayer that closes the *Aparecida Document*:

"Stay with us, for it is towards evening, and the day is now far spent."[84]

"Stay with us, Lord, keep us company, even though we have not always recognized You. Stay with us, because all around us the shadows are deepening, and You are the Light; discouragement is eating its way into our hearts: make them burn with the certainty of Easter. We are tired of the journey, but You comfort us in the breaking of bread, so that we are able to proclaim to our brothers and sisters that You have truly risen and have entrusted us with the mission of being witnesses to Your resurrection.

"Stay with us, Lord, when mists of doubt, weariness or difficulty rise up around our Catholic faith; You are Truth itself, You are the one who reveals the Father to us: enlighten our minds with Your word, and help us to experience the beauty of believing in You.

"Remain in our families, enlighten them in their doubts, sustain them in their difficulties, console them in their sufferings and in their daily labors, when around them shadows build up which threaten their unity and their natural identity. You are Life itself: remain in our homes so that they may continue to be nests where human life is generously born, where life is welcomed, loved and respected from conception to natural death.

"Remain, Lord, with those in our societies who are most vulnerable; remain with the poor and the lowly, with indigenous

---

[84] Lk. 24:29

peoples and those of African descent, who have not always found space and support to express the richness of their culture and the wisdom of their identity. Remain, Lord, with our children and with our young people, who are the hope and the treasure of our Continent; protect them from so many snares that attack their innocence and their legitimate hopes. O Good Shepherd, remain with our elderly and with our sick. Strengthen them all in faith, so that they may be Your disciples and missionaries!"[85]

---

[85] AD 554

CHAPTER TWO
LIFE[86]

Here in our midst, Jesus Christ is alive as we celebrate the Eucharist. He is the same Lord of Life who multiplied the loaves, then made His disciples set out in their boat across the Sea of Galilee to Gennesaret while He went up to the mountain to pray alone. He is the Lord who then rejoined His disciples at daybreak—walking toward them on the water.[87] Before such power we bow our believing hearts and adore Him. We unite ourselves with Him in thanksgiving as we begin this meeting that will deal with "The Family and Life, Fifty Years After the Universal Declaration of Human Rights." He is the Lord of all life. He is the Faithful Witness,[88] and He remains faithful because He cannot betray Himself.[89] He came to give life and to give it in abundance; He is "God with us." He is our companion on the journey, present at the crossroads of history, at events both great and small. That is why the Spirit moves us to confess, as did the disciples in the boat when the storm quieted down: "Truly, you are the Son of God."[90]

We too are weathering storms large and small. Our meeting today deals with one of the most dangerous storms in history. As St. John Paul II warned us, *"There seems to be a model for society today where the powerful dominate, marginalizing and even eliminating the weak. I'm referring to the unborn, helpless victims of abortion; to the incurably sick, sometimes victims of euthanasia;*

---

[86] Meeting with Latin American Politicians and Legislators, March 8, 1999.

[87] Mt. 14:15-36

[88] Rev. 1

[89] 2 Tm. 2:13

[90] Mt. 14:33

51

to the elderly, and so many other human beings marginalized by consumerism and materialism...."[91]   *"That model of society is marked by a culture of death and therefore stands in opposition to the message of the Gospel. Faced with this discouraging situation, the Church community intends to commit itself ever more completely to defending the culture of life."*[92]   This defense of the culture of life has to be carried out on all fronts, but I must remind you that life's most defensible fortress is the family, where life begins.   Today, "many are the threats to the stability of the family, and those threats are challenges for Christians."[93]

We are with Peter during that night on the lake.   On the one hand the presence of the Lord gives us the courage to accept and overcome the challenges we face; but on the other, we are threatened by the environment of self-sufficiency and of arrogance, of pure pride, that has been created by the culture of death.   We are afraid of perishing in the midst of the storm, but with the certainty that comes from the Holy Spirit, we believe that the Lord is here. Nevertheless, putting our belief in the Lord to the test are the cut-short cries of so many babies who are never born—a daily, silent, protected genocide.   The same test comes when we hear of a man or woman dying abandoned, asking only for the kind of tender caress that the culture of death can never give.   Or the multitude of families reduced to rags by consumerism and materialism.   Faced with all these contradictions, but in the presence of the glorified Jesus Christ, and united as the faithful people of God, we cry out today, as Peter did when he began to sink beneath the waves, "Lord, save me!"[94]   We stretch out our hand to grab hold of the

---

[91] EA 63

[92] *Ibid.*

[93] EA 46

[94] Mt. 14:13

Lord, the only one who can give true meaning to our helplessness in these waters.

Let us also ask our Mother, the Mother of every life and every tenderness, to show us how to build a culture of life, just as she did for the first disciples when persecutions began. And humbly asking our heavenly Father to look on our society so drenched in death, we cry out in prayer as Moses did, *Heal us, O God, we beg of you!*[95]

---

[95] See Num. 12:13. Miriam and Aaron, Moses' sister and brother, in a veiled challenge to Moses' leadership, spoke against him for marrying "outside the faith" to a Cushite woman, Sephora. God punished this challenge by inflicting on Miriam a disfiguring disease traditionally described as leprosy. Aaron asked Moses to ask the Lord to cure Miriam, which Moses did, and Miriam was cured. Moses' words are paraphrased above. (Trans. note)

CHAPTER THREE
PROTECTING THE UNBORN[96]

Mary's "Yes" was the beginning of a long journey—the journey of the Son of God among us. Today's Solemnity of the Annunciation is the real starting point of that journey of the Lord, who "went about doing good."[97] With His own wounds He healed our hurts. He proclaimed our triumph with His Resurrection. In a sense, Jesus was saving His People even while in His mother's womb. He wanted to do all that we do, even being a baby in the womb. He became a man like us in all things but sin. The Incarnation changed human existence radically. The Lord took on our life and raised it to a supernatural order. The presence of the Word of God made flesh transforms all that is human, but does not negate humanity. He elevates humanity, and places it within the Kingdom of God. In this way, the yet-unborn child Jesus brings light to the life of every person still in its mother's womb. By our faith—through the mystery of the Incarnation of the Word—what is human, what relates to the natural order, takes on a supernatural dimension that, far from denying nature, perfects nature and brings it to fulfillment.

With the Incarnation, a new perspective opens up that allows us to understand the origin and development of our life. Christ, in Mary's womb, is the key to understanding and interpreting our path, our life, and the rights of the unborn. Contemplation of Christ in his mother's womb leads us to a deeper understanding of what the natural law already tells us about the unborn.

---

[96] Homily on the Solemnity of the Annunciation, the Day of the Unborn Child in Argentina, March 25, 2004.

[97] Acts 10:38

Jesus became a baby. Jesus started out like every other baby and became part of a family. Everything that people experience when a baby is on the way—a mother's *tenderness* toward her child who is coming into the world; the *hopes* of a father (no less for being a foster father!) who is staking the future on a promise; *patient* growth, each day a little more, till birth. In Jesus, all this takes on a new meaning that illuminates our understanding of the mystery of life and seals our being with values that blossom into habits: *tenderness*, *hope* and *patience*. Without these three, *tenderness, hope* and *patience*, respect for the life and growth of the unborn is impossible. *Tenderness* makes us devoted; *hope* is a leap into the future; *patience* keeps us company through the months of waiting. These three are the setting in which the jewel of new life grows day by day.

On the other hand, when these habits are lacking, the baby becomes an "object"; the mother and father are distant; the baby is often seen as a "something," a disturbance, an intruder into the lives of adults who would rather not be bothered, imprisoned as they are in paralyzing egoism. Yet even from His mother's womb, Jesus accepts the risks of that egoism. Then once born, but still a baby, He is threatened by the persecution of that Herod who "slaughtered the innocents because he himself had been slain by the fear that was in his heart."[98] Today, too, babies and the unborn are threatened by the egoism of those whose hearts are darkened by hopelessness, the hopelessness that sows fear and reaps death. Today, too, our culture of individualism refuses to be fruitful, even while embracing a permissiveness that lowers every standard, buying barrenness with innocent blood. Today also we are under the influence of a theism that dissolves our humanity, a superficial

---

[98] Mt. 2:16-18

theism that attempts to supplant the Grand Truth that "the Word was made flesh."[99] Finally, today's culture tempts us to embrace a closed and self-involved individualism, much to the detriment of human rights and the rights of children. This is what our present-day Herods are like.

The Incarnation of the Word, Jesus the baby born from Mary's womb, calls on us, once again, to take courage. We refuse to lower ourselves by adopting a culture of superficiality that destroys us, and that—because it kills little by little—always ends up being a culture of death. We want to preach the presence of Christ, even in His Mother's womb, a presence that reaffirms the reality of every child not yet born. It is the basis for our "Yes" to life, a yes inspired by the Life that He who is our Way wished to share. In Christ, the centrality of the person as masterwork of creation is fully revealed. Appreciating this centrality, we understand more fully both the mystery of the person from the first moment of conception and the natural moral order that governs human life.

On this Solemnity of the Incarnation of the Word, I want to ask our Mother, the Virgin Mary, to put us close to Jesus; to make the habits of *tenderness*, *hope* and *patience* grow in our hearts so that we can keep safe all human life, especially the most vulnerable, marginalized and helpless. Amen.

---

[99] Jn. 1:14

CHAPTER FOUR
PARISH AND FAMILY[100]

The *Puebla Document* tells us that the parish and the family are "evangelizing centers of communion and participation."[101]

In the family and in the parish, the person is at the center of life, of the culture and of the faith, and specifically in his or her communitary dimension. Against ideological, financial and political "centers of power"[102] we place our hope in the parish and the family, which are "centers of love," rich in human warmth and based on solidarity and participation.

I want to consider this centrality for a few moments. The centrality of both the family and the parish rests in their being spaces that are always open to grace, natural cultural spaces that on our Latin American soil have had, and have been marked by, a special interrelation. The family space in the home and the ecclesial space of the parish have been intimately connected since the beginnings of our evangelization, and even before.[103] They are a common space open to grace. They stand against the centrifugal tendencies—creators of loneliness and broken relationships—that

---

[100] Presentation at the Plenary Session of the Pontifical Commission for Latin America, January 18, 2007.

[101] PD 567ff.

[102] See Paragraph 10 of the Concluding Document of the Second General Conference of the Latin American Episcopate, held in Medellín, Colombia, 1968. In this volume, the Conference is referred to as the "Medellín Conference," and the Document is referred to as the Medellín Document, cited herein as "MD." See also PD 501, 550.

[103] Taken from St. John Paul II's Message to the Amerindians, October 12, 1992, where he pointed out his appreciation for the value of the family as something very much present in the life of our indigenous peoples. (PD 17)

are characteristic of the new culture that is taking hold.[104] That is why speaking of the "centrality" of the parish and of the family is not simply a formality that lists descriptive and abstract criteria and that puts many different centers of communion and participation on the same level. The centrality of the parish and of the family is vital for the evangelization of our culture and, conversely, for the inculturation of the Gospel, which, when it is truly and designedly at the center, is able to enlighten and make fruitful the farthest reaches of the world and of culture.

Centrality of the Family

The family is the natural center of human life, which is not "individual"—it is personal/social. Any opposition between person and society is a false opposition. The one doesn't exist without complementing the other. There can be opposition between individual and societal interests, or between "global" and personal interests, but not between the two dimensions that make up the human being: the personal and the "familial-communitary-social."

For this reason, the Church meditates on the family, the foundation of personal and social life, and promotes it in its deepest values, defending it when it is attacked or denigrated. That is why the Church tries to show today's men and women that the family founded on matrimony has the two values essential for every society and for all cultures: stability and fruitfulness.[105] Many in modern societies tend to consider and to defend the rights

---

[104] "The impact of the secularized milieu has sometimes produced centrifugal tendencies in the community and the loss of an authentic ecclesial sense." (PD 627)

[105] See Cardinal Carlo Maria Martini, S.J. (1927-2012), *Family and Politics*, Speech delivered on the occasion of the Vigil of St. Ambrose, December 6, 2000, when he was Archbishop of Milan.

of the individual, and that is good. But not for that reason should we forget the importance for every society, Christian or not, of those basic roles that are found only in the family based on marriage—fatherhood, motherhood, childhood, brotherhood, sisterhood—and that are at the base of any society, and without which every society gradually becomes unstable and anarchic.

The *Puebla Document* speaks to us of the family as the center where those "four fundamental personal relations—parent, child, brother/sister and husband/wife—find their full development." And it quotes the following passage from *Gaudium et Spes*: *"These same relationships make up the life of the Church: the experience of God as Father, the experience of Christ as our brother, our experience as children in, with, and through the Son, and the experience of Christ as the spouse of the Church. Family life reproduces these four basic experiences and shares them in miniature. They are four aspects of human love."*[106]

As St. John Paul II said in one of his homilies at the Puebla Conference, the profound theological reason for being a family lies in the fact that "the family is the image of a God who 'in His most intimate mystery is not alone but is a family.'"[107] And because of this, the law of the family is "the law of conjugal love, it is communion and participation,[108] not domination."[109]

---

[106] PD 583, quoting GS 49

[107] John Paul II, *Homily at the Puebla Conference*, 2; AAS 71, 184.

[108] "In the Eucharist the family finds its full measure of communion and participation. It prepares for this through its yearning and quest for the Kingdom, purifying the soul of all that distances it from God. In the spirit of oblation, it exercises the common priesthood and participates in the Eucharist. This is prolonged in life through dialogue, in which it shares conversation, concerns, and plans, thus deepening family communion. To live the Eucharist is to recognize and share the gifts we receive from the Holy Spirit through Christ.

FAMILY AND LIFE

The revelation of the one and triune God, proclaimed by Jesus Christ, finds its best witnesses in families from all over the world. Why? Because the family is the stable and fruitful environment of free gift and love in which the Word can be welcomed and meditated on little by little and grow like a seed that becomes a great tree. Why? Because the roles that interact in the family and that are essential for personal and social life, are also essential for God: Family life allows us to receive the revelation of the family love of God in an understandable way. We take in the faith like mother's milk.[110] It was not for nothing that the path by which the Lord Himself chose to reveal Himself and save us was to "pitch His tent"[111] in human history in that first Church, that center of communion and participation—the Holy Family of Nazareth.

It is to accept the welcome we get from others and to let them come into our own lives. Once again the Spirit of the covenant surges up, as we allow God to enter our lives and use them as He sees fit. At the center of family life there emerges the strong but gentle image of the crucified and resurrected Christ." (PD 588)

[109] PD 582

[110] "In the plan of God the Creator and Redeemer, the family discovers not only its identity but also its mission: to care for, reveal and communicate love and life, through four fundamental commitments (FC 17) : a) To live, grow, and perfect itself as a community of persons that is characterized by unity and indissolubility. The family is the privileged place for personal development, together with loved ones. b) To be a 'shrine of life' (CA 39), a servant of life, because the right to life is the foundation of all human rights. This service is not reduced to just procreation, but is an efficacious help to pass on authentic human and Christian values and educate for them. c) To be 'a primary living cell of society' (FC 42). By its nature and vocation the family should be a promoter of development and advocate for appropriate family policies. d) To be a 'Domestic Church' that embraces, lives, celebrates and proclaims the Word of God. It is the shrine where holiness is built and from where the Church and the world can be made holy." (FC 55)

[111] In the Greek, $\varepsilon\sigma\kappa\eta\nu\omega\sigma\varepsilon\nu$; see Jn 1:14 (Trans. note)

Being able to live these basic relations fully is something that centers the heart and allows a person to grow in a healthy and creative way. But if in that person's heart those fundamental relations are broken, that person cannot feel him or herself part of a people, nor feel close to all, nor take account of those who are far distant and excluded, nor be open to transcendence. Starting from the loving centrality of the family, the person can grow and love, becoming open to all "peripheries,"[112] not only societal peripheries but also personal ones, where adoration of an ever-greater God begins.

Centrality of the Parish

When the *Puebla Document* highlights the great sense of family that our peoples have,[113] or when the *Santo Domingo Document*[114] tells us that "the parish, community of communities and

---

[112] "Everywhere in Latin America we can find 'homes where food and well-being are not lacking, but harmony and joy perhaps are; homes where families live rather modestly, uncertain of the morrow, helping one another to live a difficult but dignified existence; or habitations on the outskirts of your cities where there is much hidden suffering, though the simple joy of the poor dwells there; humble shanties of peasants, indigenous people, immigrants, etc.' (from the Homily of St. John Paul II at the Puebla Conference, PD 4; AAS 71, 186). We conclude by emphasizing the point that the very facts that point to the disintegration of the family end up revealing 'the true character of this institution in one way or another' (GS 47). It 'was not abolished, either by the penalty of original sin or by the punishment of the flood' (*Liturgy of Holy Matrimony*); but it continues to suffer from a hardness of the human heart (Mt. 19:8)." (PD 581)

[113] "In the great sense of family that our peoples have, the fathers of the Medellín Conference saw a primordial trait of the Latin American culture." (PD 570, quoting from St. John Paul II's *Homily at the Puebla Conference*, 2; AAS 71, 184)

[114] Message of the Fourth General Conference of the Latin American Episcopate, Santo Domingo, Dominican Republic, 1992. The Conference is referred to herein as the "Santo Domingo Conference," and the Message is referred to as the "*Santo Domingo Document*" and cited as "SDD."

movements, welcomes the anguish and hopes of humanity, and animates and gives direction to communion and participation and mission," and that "the parish is not principally a structure, a territory, a building," it is "the family of God, like a brotherhood animated by the spirit of unity,"[115] they are not talking about an abstract family or parish; they are talking about the Latin American family and parish, where the faith in Jesus Christ that continues to shine forth and give light was sown. The parish, as a privileged place of communion and participation,[116] had in Latin America a very special historic role: The very social life of our continent was a parish activity. The parish was at the center of just-founded or recently- conquered cities, or else the parish created cities where no earlier settlements existed. When San Roque Gonzalez de Santa Cruz[117] went into the missionary jungle to gather the dispersed tribes of Amerindians, he reported: *"What aroused great admiration was that the Amerindians had erected a Cross in front of the church (a tiny mud hut that the missionaries had built themselves) and, after we explained to them the reason why Christians venerate the Cross, we and they all venerated the Cross*

---

[115] SDD 58

[116] "In addition to the Christian family, which is the first center for evangelization, believers live their fraternal moments in the bosom of the local church, in communities that render the Lord's salvific design present and operative, lived out in communion and participation. Thus, within the local church we must consider the parishes, Christian base ecclesial communities, and other ecclesial groups." (PD 617)

[117] Jesuit missionary and martyr (1576-1628), born in Asunción, Paraguay, and active in what is now Paraguay, Argentina and Brazil (the Rio de La Plata Basin). He was canonized in 1988. (Trans. note)

on our knees; and even though it is the only one in these parts, I hope in the Lord that it will be followed by many others."[118]

The political and economic gestation of Latin America was dramatic, with bright spots and shadows, as the *Puebla Document* reveals.[119] There were peaceable settlements and intermarriage, as well as conquest and domination with varying degrees of violence. Nevertheless, the seed of Faith around which the spiritual life of the Latin American and Caribbean peoples is centered was sown and welcomed into the earth in that "parish" gesture that San Roque describes—when the Amerindians themselves erected a Cross in front of the chapel and all present, Amerindians and missionaries, knelt to pray together. The spatiotemporal reality around which the towns and cities began to be organized was the Cross, not a dominator's monolith. It was the chapel, built before or together with the city hall and, of course, much earlier than the banks. In that way, the history of the People of God in our land wove and shaped itself around the parish, that spiritual center which treats all of its children as equals before God the Father. The

---

[118] "The Yearly Letters of Padre Roque Gonzalez," *Documents for the History of Argentina*, vol. 12, Buenos Aires, 1929, p. 25.

[119] "The generation of peoples and cultures is always dramatic, enveloped in a mixture of light and shadow. As our human task, evangelization is subject to the vicissitudes of history; but it always tries to transfigure them with the fire of the Spirit along the way of Christ, who is the center and meaning of all history and of each and every person. Spurred on by all the contradictions and upheavals of those founding epochs, and immersed in a gigantic process of domination and cultural growth that has not yet come to an end, the evangelization that went into the making of Latin America is one of the important chapters in the history of the Church. In the face of difficulties that were both enormous and unprecedented, that evangelization responded with a creative capacity whose inspiration keeps the traditional piety of the majority of our people alive." (PD 6)

original name of each one of our towns and cities, even though certain parts were later changed, is tucked away in chapels and churches dedicated to the Lord, to our Lady, and to the patron saints of each location.

The earlier close relation between the families and the parish is still present in the villages in the interior of our countries, as well as in the collective imagination of the faithful People of God for whom, in large unplanned cities, the only visible center is often the parish Church. Our great shrines are undeniably the spatiotemporal centers in which our faithful gather in pilgrimage every year to recommit themselves; and each family does the same at the time of its special family celebrations.

Just as the family is the cultural/natural space that is open to the Faith, the parish—particularly in Latin America and the Caribbean—is the cultural/historical space that is open to the Faith. I think that the pastoral ministry at shrines, with their welcome and openness to all, with their free access and the administration of the Sacraments, and the air of celebration and brotherhood that exists in them, has much to teach every parish, which should not compete with other movements and communities but should strive to be a common space for all. That means self-denial and an attitude of service, of church-planting, without any desire for control.

The Fruits of Centrality

Why does it do us good to think about the centrality of the family and the parish? Because, as we said, the centrality of the family and of the parish (especially in *our* lands) is a concrete centrality—historical, settled, a common centrality that has given space to grace and given birth to both an evangelized culture and an inculturated way of living the Gospel. These institutions provide a place of development and service for our people that other institutions cannot.[120] Centrality produces culture, and our faith is a faith that becomes part of the culture. In addition, to become a worthwhile and lasting element of a culture, faith enters into communion with those centers in which the culture is in ferment; it takes nourishment from them, it enters into hearts, it takes on a structure. Therefore, in order to be that which they are—authentic "centers" of communion and participation—the family and the parish must nourish and cultivate the elemental graces they receive constantly from their nature and from the Spirit. In that context, from the many graces the Lord gives us, I would like to emphasize two that are irreplaceable in the family and in the parish: *Truth* and *Love*.

Spaces Open to the Word

The family and the parish are the places where the word is true, where the truth is not only discovery, it is also fidelity.

The family is, naturally, the place of the word. The family creates itself with fundamental words of love, with that "I do" that establishes a covenant between the husband and wife forever. "In the family, a newborn opens itself to the meaning of words thanks to the affection and smiles of its mother and father, and it finds the courage to speak. In the family, the word is identified with the person who speaks it and all have a voice: children, young people, adults and the elderly. In the family the word can be trusted because it holds the memory of affectionate gestures and

---

[120] "We must stress a more determined option for an overall coordinated pastoral effort, with the collaboration of religious communities in particular. We must promote groups, communities, and movements, inspiring them to an ongoing commitment to communion. We must turn the parish into a center for promoting services that smaller communities cannot surely provide." (PD 650)

accompanies new acts of affection every day. This point can be summarized by saying that the family is the place of the word because it is centered on love. Words said and listened to in the family never disappear; they circle around the heart, illuminating it, guiding it, giving it encouragement. A father's advice, the prayer learned from reading a mother's lips, a secret shared with a brother or sister, the stories told by grandparents—these are the words that make up the little universe that every heart treasures.

The parish is also a place of the Word. It has been so from the moment that the Word, incarnated in the Holy Family of Nazareth, wished to open Itself to the wider community by reading the word in the synagogue of Nazareth. The parish is, indeed must be, the environment in which the unfathomable richness of the Word that dwells in the Church becomes understandable in the daily life of every town, of every community.

The parish is one of the few places where mothers and fathers can go with their children to listen to the same Word. At schools, parents must leave their children off; but at Sunday Mass, parents and children can all go together and be enlightened by the same Word. Other places of the word—the "media"—are precisely that: "means." In the family and in the parish, the Word is life—gesture, constancy, love shown, truth lived, reliable faithfulness.[121]

Spaces Open to Love

The other grace is about love and has to do with the acceptance of the other, freely given, forgiving and creative. It has to do with

---

[121] "This evangelization will have its renewing force in fidelity to the Word of God, its place of reception in the ecclesial community, its creative breath in the Holy Spirit, who creates in unity and diversity, who increases charismatic and ministerial richness and who projects itself into the world by means of a missionary commitment." (SDD 27)

the inclusion of all.[122] The family and the parish are places of refuge, of communion in deep love, more so than other areas of life where change is constant.

Often parents get very worried when that see that their children don't share their values. This can be true at a certain level: present-day society makes available many things that previously were provided by the family (and by the school) and that can now be obtained elsewhere. The centrality of the family in the privacy of its home, the simple joys around the dinner table, the home as the place where sickness is cared for and where we take our rest, where we can reveal who we are and be accepted for it: These values remain valid and vital for every human heart. The four relations of which we have spoken (husband/wife, fatherhood/motherhood, childhood, brother-/sisterhood) make up the family. They are the base values for all other values. They can be developed as much by translating them into practices and customs accepted by all of society (as was the case in earlier cultures) as by contrasting them with certain environments that can be fascinating but lack those basic values and the warmth they provide.

In the same way, the parish continues to be the center of the life of our people, even if statistical studies show that participation

---

[122] "The life of communion of the disciples of Jesus Christ is a gift that shows the unity by means of the diversity and plurality of the nations, tongues, races and customs: remembering that it is the image of the one and triune God. When in the Church love is lived, the differences never divide; instead, they enrich the unity, centered around the Pope, successor of Peter and pastor of the universal Church. This communion is found in dioceses, around the bishop, and it is lived in the parishes and their communities, without forgetting the family, the Domestic Church, the place where for the first time we live and learn the gratuitousness of love and the joy of communion" (Preparatory Document to the Aparecida Conference, no. 71).

in certain ceremonies and traditions is decreasing. People judge the parish on whether it promotes those basic family relationships: Do we baptize their children, bless their marriages, visit their sick, comfort families when they bury their dead, welcome the poor as brothers, keep the door open like a merciful father for all our children, both prodigal and obedient? The parish makes everyone equal because it brings all the outlying areas to the center of ecclesial life: poverty, marginality, absence of political, financial, and social influence, and the extremes of life—birth and death, sin and grace.

The Challenge of Evangelization of Culture and of Inculturation of the Gospel

I would describe the challenge we are facing in the new evangelization of culture and the inculturation of the Gospel in this way: It is the challenge of recentering ourselves on Christ and on our culture—on our cultures—in order to reach all the outlying areas, the peripheries. It is not a question of "forgetting about the first evangelization," nor of "preaching a different Gospel," nor of thinking that the earlier preaching was not fruitful. It is rather a question of the new challenges of today's cultures.[123]

---

[123] "The new evangelization has as its point of departure the certitude that in Christ there are inscrutable riches (Eph. 3:8) which do not exhaust any culture, any age, which we can have recourse to for our own enrichment" (John Paul II, Inaugural Address, 6).

"To speak of the New Evangelization is to recognize that there existed an earlier or first evangelization. It would be improper to speak of a new evangelization of tribes or peoples who have never heard the Gospel. In Latin America we can speak of a New Evangelization because there was a first evangelization five hundred years ago." (SDD 24)

Centering Ourselves on the Communitary Dimension of the Person

In Germany in 2005, Cardinal Errázuriz said that the center of that year's Königstein Conference was not "primarily a grand program: the new evangelization, the Christian culture and human development," but rather a program "centered on that baptized person who is going to forge the Christian culture, who must be an evangelizer and work for the benefit of his or her brothers and sisters, especially the most marginalized. It is a new perspective on education in the faith. It is about being and forming disciples and missionaries of Jesus Christ."[124]

I would like to place this person—this "disciple and missionary of Jesus Christ" whom we want to go forth to evangelize "so that our people have life in Him"—squarely in the framework of what St. John Paul II suggested in his Inaugural Address at the Santo Domingo Conference: *"To the troubling phenomenon of the sects, one has to respond with pastoral action that puts the person, including his communitary dimension and his desire for a personal relationship with God, at the center. It is a fact that where the presence of the Church is dynamic—as in the case of parishes where a devoted catechesis of the Word of God is imparted, where there exists an active and participative liturgy, a solid Marian piety, an effective solidarity in social matters, a marked pastoral concern for the family, the youth and the sick— we see that neither sects nor parareligious movements take root or develop."*[125]

The remedy that the Pope counsels with respect to the corrosive action of sects is inspired: Put the person, and his

---

[124] Cardinal Francisco Javier Errázuriz Ossa, now Archbishop Emeritus of Santiago, Chile, was President of CELAM at the time (2005) of the Königstein Conference.

[125] Santo Domingo Conference, Inaugural Discourse of the Holy Father, 6.

openness to community and to the transcendent, at the center of everything. It is for this reason that we consider the remedy proposed by St. John Paul II to be not only an appropriate response to the sects, but also an effective way to combat an aspect of globalization that tends to eliminate communitary values and institutions in order to deal with persons as isolated—hence more easily manipulated—individuals, to the benefit of both consumerism and crony politics. The family and the parish are ideal communitary environments for promoting a person-culture-faith relationship to protect against this danger.

Concentrating on Our Cultural Core

Faced as we are with the "cultural crisis of unexpected proportions" in which we live, and faced with the breakdown of the relationship between Gospel values and culture,[126] we can be guided by St. John Paul II's description, in his Santo Domingo Inaugural Address, of evangelization aimed at our cultural core: *"Our times require a special effort and sensitivity in order to inculturate the message of Jesus in such a way that Christian values can transform the various core elements of culture, purifying them if necessary and making possible the consolidation of a Christian culture that can renew, extend, and unify past and present historic values in order to respond adequately to present-day challenges."*[127]

---

[126] See Blessed Paul VI: "The division between the Gospel and culture is without a doubt the drama of our time, just as it was of other times. Therefore every effort must be made to ensure a full evangelization of culture, or more correctly, of cultures. They have to be regenerated by an encounter with the Gospel. But this encounter will not take place if the Gospel is not proclaimed." (EN 20)

[127] RM 52

In 1992, St. John Paul II clarified the notion of penetrating to the core of a culture by stating that the evangelization of culture is in no way a merely exterior adaptation. It is a radical taking hold of the cultural processes of peoples and of their deeply rooted understanding of their worlds.[128] And this deeply rooted understanding needs broader and more lasting "space" than any one individual consciousness can provide. That is why the family and the parish are important: They are "spaces" where the historical and present values of our culture and our faith can be strengthened, renewed, broadened and unified.

The Circularity of Our Culture

The "center" is a profoundly constituent element of our Latin American culture, a culture that is strongly "circular." Remembering this helps us understand things that can't be understood if one begins from a linear, rationalistic concept that says progress requires the emergence of new things that have nothing to do with the old. This mentality is evident in the dissatisfaction that some feel seeing that "we're making no progress," or that "the past returns with its ghosts and its same bad habits" (as if the new were better just because it's new). Latin

---

[128] "The evangelization of culture is an effort to understand the mentality and attitudes of the contemporary world and to shine the light of the Gospel on them. Its intent is to reach all levels of human life in order to make it more worthy" (*Address to the World of Culture*, Lima, May 15, 1988). However, "this effort at understanding and shedding light must always be accompanied by the proclamation of the Good News" (*Redemptoris Missio*, 46). Thus, the Gospel's penetration of cultures will not be a mere external adaptation, but a "profound and all-embracing one, which involves the Christian message and also the Church's reflection and practice" (*Ibid.* 52), and which "always respects the characteristics and integrity of the faith." (Santo Domingo Conference, Inaugural Discourse of the Holy Father, 22).

American culture and faith have been created from and revolve around specific centers of communion and participation: spatial centers, like shrines, and temporal centers, like the great feasts, in which communion and participation reach their greatest splendor. Our people moves forward, pilgrims in time and in geography around these major centers, while "living in" smaller centers like the family and the parish. Taking responsibility for them, developing them, reflecting on their meaning and enhancing the graces of these centers is the same as taking responsibility for, developing and enhancing our very culture and faith themselves.

The Center as the Condition for Stability and Fruitfulness.

We know that individual cultures develop out of the way peoples create centers and expand them based on their values, whether everyday, esthetic, ethical/political or transcendent. Every culture first centers itself where it can do the work necessary to make possible the life it desires. Every culture then centers itself in time, setting a rhythm of life with its expansions and contractions according to the seasons, the climate, its work, celebration and rest, all consistent with each people's beliefs. This centering is spiritual, but not in a restrictive sense, rather in the sense that the spirit centers everything that is human—body and soul, person and society, things and values, moments and history: everything.

Every people transforms the places and times that it encounters and, on the basis of its own spirit, configures them to what it desires, to what it remembers, and to what it plans. And it accomplishes this centering not as individuals, but in the family, the parish, the town. Centering is a necessary precondition for the birth and life of a culture because from that center comes the culture's stability and fruitfulness.

Centering Ourselves on Jesus Christ

St. John Paul II concluded his Inaugural Message at the Santo Domingo Conference with a beautiful exhortation to turn our gaze toward our center. He speaks to Latin America and to the people of the Caribbean as if he were speaking to Our Lady: *"What was spoken to you by the Lord will be fulfilled. Be faithful to your baptism, reawaken in this [Columbus] Quincentenary the immense grace you have received, rest your heart. Turn your gaze toward the center, the beginning, to Him who is the basis of every happiness, the fullness of all things! Open yourself to Christ, welcome the Spirit so that there is a new Pentecost in all your communities! A new, happy humanity will arise from you and you will feel again the powerful hand of the Lord, and the words of the Lord shall be fulfilled. What He professed to you, America, is His love for you, and His love for all humankind, for your families, for your peoples. This love will be fulfilled in you, and you will find yourself again, you will find your countenance. All generations shall call you blessed."*[129]

We see that the challenge of announcing Jesus Christ to our peoples—not to isolated individuals—so that in Him they have life—a full life, in all the dimensions of their culture—carries with it the task of recentering. Recentering on Jesus Christ, who already dwells at the center of our culture and who comes to us, always new, from that center. This contemplation, which always recenters on a living Christ, who lives in the midst of His faithful people, frees us from the linear and abstract temptations of those who think that the Gospel has to be brought up to date. Some, for example, want it

---

[129] Lk. 1:48; *Ibid.* 31

"restored" like a piece of antique furniture; others want to rewrite it as the constitution for yet another proposed Utopia.[130] Recentering ourselves means having the courage to remember, arriving at our culture's most ancient memories, and recognizing in them, gratefully, the presence of the Spirit. Recentering ourselves means having the courage to strike out into the uncharted land of the future, trusting that the Lord will come to us, full of glory and might.

---

[130] See Bergoglio, *Meditations for Religious,* Ed. Diego de Torres, Buenos Aires, 1982, pp. 54-55.

CHAPTER FIVE
TRADITIONAL PIETY AS
INCULTURATION OF THE FAITH[131]

The Aparecida Conference was an ecclesial happening that looked carefully at Latin American reality and called on the Church to fulfill its evangelizing mission.

The Spirit of Aparecida

It was nothing new for the Church to make evangelization the goal of its activity. The Church's original and basic task is to proclaim salvation to all peoples.[132]

But the urgent call to evangelization that came from the Aparecida Conference was based on the perception that Latin American Catholicism was "wearing out." Over more than five hundred years, Christianity has penetrated the cultures of Latin America and has offered a piety that nourishes the lives of our peoples when it is welcomed sincerely. Nevertheless, even though Catholics are still in the majority, something is changing. As Pope (now Emeritus) Benedict XVI acknowledged at the beginning of the Conference, *"It is true that one can detect a certain weakening of Christian life in society overall and of participation in the life of the Catholic Church due to secularism, hedonism, indifferentism and*

---

[131]   First published on January 19, 2008 in *La religiosidad popular como inculturación de la fe* CELAM -SECRETARÍA GENERAL, Testigos de Aparecida, II, Bogotá, CELAM, 2008, pp. 281-325. Updated in that volume to take into account subsequent relevant Papal documents. (Trans. note)

[132] Mt. 28:19

proselytism by numerous sects, animist religions and new pseudo-religious phenomena."[133]

We are in a new epoch, undergoing profound and accelerated changes. This situation gives rise to uncertainty, confusion, and fear in the hearts of the men and women of our time. In the Latin American and Caribbean context, change becomes more complex and dramatic because our peoples live in circumstances where poverty and exclusion are growing, where institutionalized corruption is pervasive, and where violence of all kinds is increasing while personal identity is more and more lost.

This situation has been caused by changes that were foreseen by the Second Vatican Council some forty years ago.[134] Those transformations have accelerated and increased, and with the changing times we need a new way to place ourselves in a history that has changed and will continue to change. We are seeing things we thought would never happen, at least not in our time, and the future looks hazy.

The phenomena that have emerged in postmodernity, the effects of globalization, and many other processes cannot be minimized by thinking that we are just facing a temporary crisis and that all we have to do is wait until things go back to the way they were. Globalization is unjust in many ways, but if it is viewed as "a network of relationships that extends over the whole planet [and that] from certain points of view...benefits the great family of humanity and is a sign of humanity's deep desire for unity,"[135] it offers a unique opportunity for the whole world to be evangelized, and for the Church to bring about the unity of the continents and

---

[133] AD 2

[134] GS 4-10

[135] Benedict XVI, Inaugural Discourse, 2.

their peoples, and to make Christian cooperation and credibility more real.

The strong conviction coming from the Aparecida Conference was that being a Christian means being a missionary and that this necessary commitment cannot be lived out in fullness and truth without a disciple's heart—a personal encounter with Christ in the community of believers. We Christians are disciples of the Master, and for that reason we cannot look at reality other than through the eyes of a missionary.

We are not impartial observers. Rather, we are men and women who want to make all societal structures fruitful with the love that we have come to know and that, as it touches the reality of the world, is able to transform that reality into abundant life.

The *Aparecida Document* says that meeting Jesus is "the best thing that has happened in our lives,"[136] that proclaiming Him fully "is what we have to offer to the world, and that resisting the culture of death with the Christian culture of solidarity is a duty incumbent on every one of us."[137]

In a concrete way, with openness that is critical, wise and prophetic, with closeness and with discernment, the Church in Latin America and the Caribbean wants to be a "missionary disciple" so that it can "give life to our peoples" in Christ.

Characteristic of a disciple is a "humble manner"[138] and "careful listening."[139] The disciple, because he is not the Master, does not even know what he is to do. He listens, he waits, he makes no reply. That is the Church of the *Aparecida Document*:   a

---

[136] AD 29

[137] AD 480

[138] AD 36

[139] AD 366

community of missionary disciples who want to listen to the Lord. Listening to the Lord is also accomplished by listening to reality with a humble spirit in order to discern what one must be and do.

Cardinal Paul Poupard, President of the Pontifical Council for Culture, has pointed out that Latin America, like the rest of the world, is experiencing a cultural transformation and that the *Aparecida Document* "is trying to establish criteria for evangelizing culture, and for determining how the Good News can be brought to differing peoples through their own cultures."[140]

The Road Traveled

An examination of the status of evangelization in Latin America today is impossible without taking into account certain concepts and expressions, "culture," "inculturation," and "traditional piety."[141] The realities that are hidden within each of these expressions have been studied and analyzed, and are the result of experience accumulated throughout history; and history itself, during its constant ups and downs, has continued to fix the meanings of these terms and the way they are used.

In the *Aparecida Document*, the word "culture" is used approximately seventy times, and the way it is used is completely different from the way it was used in the 1950's at the First General Conference of the Latin American Bishops in Rio de Janeiro. Likewise, "traditional piety" has an influence and a positive connotation that is significantly different from what could be inferred when this same term appeared in the earliest writings of the Latin American Church.

---

[140] http://www.panoramacatolico.com/antiguo/pc/20070603/fecultura.htm
[141] Translation of "*religiosidad popular*" in this volume. (Trans. note)

We cannot arrive at a complete understanding of these terms if we do not read them in the light of the history that developed them and gave them the meanings they have today. Neither can we understand the evolution of the Church in Latin America without taking into account the social and political changes that took place in that region beginning in the 1960's.

By the time the Council of Trent ended, in 1563, America had already received hundreds of missionaries and had witnessed the great controversy initiated by Bartholomé de las Casas with respect to the methods of evangelization and conversion. The continent numbered approximately thirty dioceses and had held several local and provincial councils to discuss missionary activity in America.

The following four centuries ended with the Second Vatican Council, which revealed the diversity of situations and cultures in which the Church is active. Among others, there was arthritic European Christianity, the Churches of the East (ecclesial communities in India, Japan and China), young Churches in Africa, and the populist Catholicism of Latin America.

For the first time, those situations and cultures entered "by the wide gate" and gave our local Churches a new light in which to confront old problems and begin a cultural dialogue, both internal and external. *"The Church, therefore, exhorts her children, that through dialogue and collaboration with the followers of other religions, carried out with prudence and love and in witness to the Christian faith and life, they recognize, preserve and promote the good things, spiritual and moral, as well as the sociocultural values found among these persons."*[142]

---

[142] NA 2

Elsewhere, the Second Vatican Council rediscovered the importance of charisms within the Church[143] and called for discernment of the signs of the times.[144] The Council represented an openness to dialogue with the contemporary world, a certain reconciliation with enlightened modernity and a recovery of the prophetic dimension of the Church in society. In the light of the Council's teachings, we can understand what had happened within the Church and what the Church had experienced in Latin America in the decades leading up to the Council.

a) The Medellín Conference

The Second Vatican Council discussed a wide range of subjects, but the ones that received the most attention in Latin America and the Caribbean after the Council were poverty and the need for freedom.

The Fidel Castro revolution in Cuba, the attempt to introduce developmentalism, and the populist social movements in Peru, Chile, Bolivia and Mexico brought change to the landscape in Latin America. All these, together with the failed attempt of "Che" Guevara to spread revolution from Bolivia to all of Latin America, are the context in which the 1968 Medellín Conference was held. It was not simply an application of the Council to Latin America; it was a creative re-reading of the Second Vatican Council in a world of unjust poverty and with sinful economic and social structures. The Church in Latin America began to try to understand itself and discover its mission by listening to the cry of the poor, and seeing the suffering of the people, of indigenous populations, workers, farmers and children.

---

[143] LG 12

[144] GS 4, 11, 44

Even though the question of culture was never dealt with directly at the Medellín Conference, all its reflections were tinged with the color that culture was absorbing from social reality.

The Conference took the side of the great mass of the poor in Latin America and invested a great deal of its energies in constructing a "Church born of the people," a place for the poorest to meet in order to hear and understand the word of God in the light of an awareness of everyday reality.

It was through their option for the poorest that the local churches made more direct contact with the multifaceted religious and cultural reality of this continent. In making room for the poor and letting them speak, a "hidden" Church—embracing the remembrances of 2,600 native peoples, with countless languages and traditions, as well as two million descendants of Africans—was discovered. It was inevitable that the cultural expressions of those enormous segments of the population would be introduced into the liturgy.

The Medellín Conference was so important for Latin America, and for the universal Church as well, that when the President of CELAM, Bishop (later Cardinal) Eduardo Pironio, traveled to Rome in 1974 for the Synod on Evangelization, he took with himself three pastoral ideas from Medellín that later had a significant influence on the well-known Apostolic Exhortation of Blessed Paul VI "*Evangelii Nuntiandi.*" The three ideas were: Christian base communities, liberation, and traditional piety.

b) The Puebla Conference

When the Puebla Conference convened in 1979, the process of "giving the Word back" to the poor was fully under way. Christian base communities and populist liberation movements believed that social change would be possible only if it were adopted by the masses, and those groups advocated using terminology the people were familiar with. This belief, with its lights and shadows, contributed to the Church's more programmatic re-encounter with original native cultures and people of African descent.

In the *Puebla Document*, the question of culture entered through the door of traditional piety and stayed to be included among the matters discussed at the Santo Domingo Conference. That Conference celebrated the quincentenary of the arrival of Christianity in the New World. The *Puebla Document* reflected broadly on traditional piety, but in the end dealt with it only as an imperfect realization of the "deep Catholic roots" of South America.

After 1989 the social and ecclesial landscape changed significantly. The fall of socialism in Eastern Europe, the affirmation of economic neoliberalism[145] as the only path to salvation, and the advent of cultural postmodernity brought a new perspective to the Latin American social and ecclesial awareness.

c) The Santo Domingo Conference

The challenge of inculturating the Gospel into society calls for the laity not to limit itself to intra-Church activities but rather to "penetrate socialcultural environments to become leaders in transforming society in the light of the Gospel." The laity must stop being "sacristy Christians" in their parishes and instead commit

---

[145] An economic theory described as promoting free markets, reduced government social spending, deregulation, privatization and individual responsibility as opposed to solidarity.
See, for example, http://www.corpwatch.org/article.php?id=376 and https://en.wikipedia.org/wiki/Neoliberalism. Other terms for the theory are more common. (Trans. note)

themselves to building up society in its political, economic, employment-related, cultural and environmental manifestations.

In this context, the Santo Domingo Conference, in 1992, examined the conditions for a broader understanding of Latin American cultures. There was discussion of the "unity and plurality of indigenous, African-origin, and mixed-race cultures," and progress was made in this area by recognizing Latin America to be "multiethnic and multicultural" with a "global vision that embraces all peoples" and "that seeks unity on the basis of Catholic identity."[146] Cultural and social pluralism is thus acceptable as long as it does not imply pluralism with respect to religion.

The conclusions of the Santo Domingo Conference reveal a still-open wound in the relations between Christian churches and the ancestral traditions of the population groups in Latin America: The search for and preservation of "Catholic identity" seems to conflict with the challenge of ecumenical and interreligious dialogue. The Commission 26, which met during the Conference, affirmed the "uninterrupted action of God by means of His Spirit, in all cultures,[147] understanding inculturation as "a process that begins within each people and community."[148]

In the final version of the *Santo Domingo Document*, a call was issued for the Church to *"promote an inculturation of the liturgy, embracing with appreciation the symbols, rites and religious expressions of the people with a clear sense of faith, while maintaining the value of universal symbols in harmony with the general discipline of the Church."*[149]

---

[146] SDD 244

[147] SDD225-1

[148] SDD225-2

[149] SDD248

Culture in the *Aparecida Document*

There is no doubt that the new approach to the Latin American reality adopted in the *Aparecida Document* has given special prominence to the concept of culture as an important key to interpreting that reality. There were very varied approaches to the theme, but there was no precise definition of "culture." Particular aspects of the concept do appear, however, from the document's consideration of the current situation: "New actors are emerging within the situation of cultural change, with new lifestyles, ways of thinking, feeling and perceiving, and with new ways of relating. They are authors and agents of the new culture."[150]

We are dealing with a dynamic concept that presupposes the need to speak of subjects who create and implement culture as well as of their modes of behavior and the way they describe their surroundings. This bond between culture and those who produce it gives rise to constant change in society. The various elements of culture affect each other, thus developing new forms of individual expression and decision.

The *Aparecida Document* highlights the fact that social phenomena manifest themselves with great complexity. There are situations that are recognized as unworthy of human beings, and it is necessary to discover how Christianity interacts with these situations. The Church is no longer seen to be marginal to the creation of meaning but rather as one of the agents of this process. It is not an outside critic; rather, it is an active participant in setting the structure of common spaces. That location keeps the Church from being tempted to consider itself a reality that is outside of society and all its contradictions. The Church produces culture

---

[150] AD 51

(that is, human behaviors) and it is a promoter of processes. It is only one part of a great spectrum; it is not the only agent. The influence that it has is challenged by the difficult task of convincing people that Christianity is meaningful and possible, a reality that brings humankind, and the history in which it acts every day, to its full development.

One of the basic elements in the *Aparecida Document* is its awareness of the responsibility that we have to show that the Gospel of Jesus is a true path to salvation. The other side of this coin is the need to discover and recognize the kind of role the Church has played, and must continue to play, in the face of the painful and unjust realities that afflict a significant portion of society. The *Aparecida Document* has pointed out a gap between faith and the practical social life of believers, even though many believers have carried out significant activities in support of solidarity. It is the laity who have the task of witnessing the presence of God in any given commitment to the transformation of social structures. *"The greed of the market unleashes the desires of children, youth and adults. Advertising creates the illusion of distant make-believe worlds where every desire can be satisfied by products that work, are fashionable and are "must haves." It becomes acceptable to think that the satisfaction of our desires will produce happiness. Since only the here-and-now is needed, happiness is sought through economic well-being and hedonistic satisfaction."* [151]

The fundamental cause of this breakdown is a perception that reality is completely tied up with personal satisfaction. This breakdown is clearly hastened by media that answer only to the demands of the market. The notion of happiness as the satisfaction

---

[151] AD 50

of desire is at the center of human needs. It is nothing more than self-referential narcissism. All of that is in conflict with the various situations of marginalization and suffering that characterize South America. New generations that have grown up in a climate of pragmatic individualism and self-worship are the ones most affected by these changes. For them, the past is not something they miss, and the future is uncertain. Obtaining maximum satisfaction is the reference point for their present reality, and it is what lets them forget, even if just for a while, the great conflicts and uncertainties they suffer. They live in a world in which abundance has given rise to behaviors that do not take social concerns into account.

Still, at the root of society's lack of concern for life is the depth of its disillusionment, to which must be added the phenomenon of globalization, especially in its economic aspects, which affects all sectors, putting at risk the means of subsistence of many people and, at the same time, allowing the influence of new uses and customs that generate syncretistic ideas and ambiguous behaviors, and that clash with the ways that people raised in different cultures look at things and feel about them. These clashes have brought about a new society, one in which change is a constant reality.

All of this helps us understand that ecclesial life is confronting a series of challenges in the face of which the document calls for a life of faith that makes evident the human richness of the Gospel message. The community of faith—which joins people together in a new way and, as a result, becomes a countercultural space—opposes a vision of social life centered on consumption as a certain and safe path to happiness. For a long time we have been witnessing "cultural colonization" accomplished through the imposition of artificial cultures, which give little value to local cultures and try to impose a homogenized culture that generally leads to a lack of concern for others "whom one does not need and for whom one does not feel responsible."[152] Excessive insistence on individual and subjective rights goes hand in hand with a lack of committed work for solidary social and cultural rights; and everyone's dignity is diminished, especially the dignity of the poorest and most needy. In this cultural context, our challenge is to dialogue empathetically with the different elements of a culture to create an effective way of getting close to Jesus. Lack of critical reflection and discernment can lead to a fundamentalist religious subjectivism or to the syncretism of Christians who are superficial and uninvolved. In this sense, the Aparecida Conference firmly pointed out the need for a formation of all the faithful—not an indoctrination, but rather a greater awareness on the path of faith—a formation that must go hand in hand with the human process of personal growth.

Culture and Inculturation

According to the Second Vatican Council, culture, subjectively speaking, "indicates everything whereby the person develops and perfects his or her many bodily and spiritual qualities."[153] Objectively, "culture" includes the cultivation of three basic human relationships: (a) our relationship with nature—to modify it, to rule it, and to get from it consumer goods and services; (b) our relationship with others, in order to make life together more human by improving customs and institutions; and (c) our relationship with God through the practice of religion.[154] Part of

---

[152] AD 46

[153] GS 53

[154] *Ibid.*

every culture is the way a people, through its values or anti-values, professes or denies a religious bond with God.[155]

It follows that human culture necessarily has an historical and social aspect, and the word "culture" often takes on the sociological and ethnological sense in which *"we speak of a plurality of cultures. Different styles of life and multiple scales of values arise from the diverse manner of using things, of working, of expressing oneself, of practicing religion, of forming customs, of establishing laws and legal institutions, of cultivating the sciences, the arts and beauty. Thus the customs handed down to each human community form the patrimony proper to that community."*[156] This thought was the subject of reflection in the Puebla Conference.[157]

Evangelizing Culture

On the road that has been traveled, an important milestone was the Synod of Bishops on Evangelization, which was held in Rome in 1974 and led to the Post-Synodal Apostolic Exhortation *Evangelii Nuntiandi* of Blessed Paul VI.[158] This document guided the work of the Puebla Conference.

If culture became part of the formal teaching of the magisterium of the Church for the first time in the documents of the Second Vatican Council, with the statement in *Gaudium et Spes* that "The person comes to a true and full humanity only through culture,"[159] each culture having its own value and a legitimate autonomy,[160] it was only in *Evangelii Nuntiandi*, with its

---

[155] PD 386, 389

[156] GS 53

[157] PD 387

[158] December 8, 1975

[159] GS 53

[160] GS 56; AA 7

consideration of present-day crises and its acknowledgment of the undeniable gap between Gospel and culture, that the notion of evangelization of culture and cultures appeared.[161]

The Pope and the *Puebla Document* teach that "evangelizing means bringing the Good News into all strata of humanity and, through its influence, transforming humanity from within,"[162] including the "values, points of interest, lines of thought, sources of inspiration and models of life that are in contrast with the Word of God and the plan of salvation."[163] *Gaudium et Spes* teaches that *"what matters is to evangelize culture and cultures (not in a purely decorative way, as it were, by applying a thin veneer, but in a vital way, in depth and down to their very roots), in the wide and rich sense which these terms have in Gaudium et Spes,*[164] *always taking the person as the starting point and always coming back to the relationships of persons among themselves and with God."*[165]

The *Puebla Document* gives significant consideration to this theme,[166] saying that evangelization means reaching down to the roots of cultures, transforming structures and social environments, strengthening the authentic values of cultures, contributing to the development of the "seeds of the Word,"[167] purifying negative

---

[161] EN 20

[162] EN 18

[163] EN 19

[164] GS 50

[165] EN 20

[166] PD 385-456

[167] "Seeds of the Word" is a very ancient expression, coined by Justin Martyr, c. 150 A.D., which reappeared in the documents of the Second Vatican Council to designate whatever is "true and holy" even in non-Christian religions. For a discussion of "seeds of the Word" in the context of Christology, see the Address delivered by Sandro Magister in Tokyo on June 18, 2003, "John Paul II and the Other Religions: From Assisi to *Dominus Iesus,"* available on the web at

values, eliminating idolatries and absolutized values, correcting not only false ideas about God but also eliminating the exploitation of one person by another.

A specific aspect of the evangelization of culture in Latin America is the Gospel's purification and invigoration of populist Catholicism,[168] as well as the promotion of the human person in accordance with the social teaching of the Church, so as to free us from slavery to personal and social sin and arrive at a life in community that is worthy of the children of God.[169]

The Puebla Conference developed a reflection on culture from Gaudium et Spes and assimilated the message of *Evangelii Nuntiandi* on evangelization of culture, transforming it into a pastoral program for the Church in Latin America: the Gospel must penetrate the values and criteria that inspire our cultures.[170]

According to the *Puebla Document*, there is in Latin America "a Catholic substratum ..."[171] "... of a culture suffused with faith that manifests itself in the religious attitudes of the people."[172] "Traditional piety is a treasury of values that respond with wisdom to the great questions of human existence,"[173] but today "traditional piety is threatened by urbanization, secularism and the structures of injustice that have been imposed upon it."[174]

The importance that the *Puebla Document* gives to socioeconomic structures as an element of culture and an object of

---

http://chiesa.espresso.repubblica.it/articolo/19632?eng=y (Trans. note)

[168] PD 457

[169] PD 472-506

[170] PD 395

[171] PD 7

[172] PD 413

[173] PD 448

[174] PD 37

evangelization is a great contribution to, and progress in, understanding the concept of "culture" in *Gaudium et Spes* and the challenges to evangelization pointed out in *Evangelii Nuntiandi.*

Inculturation of Faith

From a sociological perspective the expression "inculturation" denotes "the process of transmission and communication through codes, both linguistic and iconic, of the values, norms and patterns of behavior of a given social-cultural group to new generations. It is the process by which an individual receives, assimilates, reinterprets and actively adopts the culture into which he or she is born or of which he or she effectively begins to be a part."[175] Inculturation has always been a part of the Church's missionary endeavors. St. Paul put it into practice in the Greek and Roman worlds: "I became all things to all so as to be able to proclaim the Good News."[176] The work of the great missionaries in all times has been characterized by the process of inculturation. The brothers Cyril and Methodius took the light of the Gospel to the Slavic peoples and composed liturgical texts for them that were consonant with the Slavic mentality and language: "Making use of their own Greek language and culture for this arduous and unusual enterprise, they set themselves to understanding and penetrating the language, customs and traditions of the Slavic peoples, faithfully interpreting the aspirations and human values which were present and expressed therein."[177]   In the seventeenth century, the Jesuit apostles of China, Matteo Ricci and Martino

---

[175] Brazilian bishop Antônio Do Carmo Cheuiche, O.C.D. (1927-2009), "The Current Frame of Reference for the Question of Inculturation in Medellín," 60.

[176] 1 Cor 9:22-23

[177] SA 10

Martini, were able to incorporate Chinese and Malabar rituals into Catholic liturgy. In Paraguay during the first Evangelization, the Franciscan Luis Bolaños wrote the first grammar, the first dictionary, and a prayer book in Guaraní; later, Blessed José de Anchieta of the Society of Jesus studied Tupí and wrote the first grammar of that language, as well as a catechism and poems and hymns for evangelization.

When the *Puebla Document* notes some criteria for the assimilation of cultures, it speaks of an incarnation,[178] but it does not develop the question of inculturation of the Gospel. It was St. John Paul II who, in the Post-Synodal Apostolic Exhortation *Catechesi Tradendae* of 1979, officially recognized the word "inculturation" and consecrated it by explaining its meaning and giving it a universal scope. When speaking or writing about evangelization, inculturation was one of the themes he dealt with most frequently, calling it one of the important aspects of evangelization. Just a few months after the beginning of his pontificate, on April 27, 1979, he stated that "inculturation is a component of the Incarnation": that is to say, the inculturation of faith and of the Gospel is a practical consequence of the Incarnation of the Son of God, who, saving all and only those whom He welcomes,[179] properly welcomes into the Church all cultures, purifying or eliminating what is contrary to His spirit, but at the same time keeping all that is good from complete self-elimination. Inculturation is the penetration of the Gospel message into cultures, in the same way the Word became flesh and dwelt amongst us.[180]

---

[178] PD 400

[179] "*quod non est assumptum non est redemptum,*" cf. St. Gregory the Theologian (Nazianzen) (329-390), Letter to the priest Cledonius, Ep. 101 (PG 37, 181)

[180] John 1:14

Traditional Piety as Inculturation of the Faith

In his 1979 Encyclical *Redemptor Hominis*, St. John Paul II begins his anthropological discourse on the person. Men and women in the fullness of their personal—but at the same time communitary and social—being, is the obligatory road that the Church must travel in fulfillment of its mission ... a way pointed out by Christ Himself, that inevitably follows the path of Incarnation and Redemption.[181] Speaking at the United Nations Educational, Scientific and Cultural Organization (UNESCO) in Paris in 1980, he stated that "one has to affirm mankind for itself, not for another motive or reason, only for itself." He then continues, "We live a truly human life thanks to culture." Through it, the person, as person, becomes more a person. In a 1982 talk to pilgrims from Bergamo, Italy, speaking about Christian culture and the evangelization of culture, the pope stated the fundamental understandings that would guide his magisterium: a healthy anthropological understanding of culture, and a theological understanding of inculturation of the Gospel.

It is through culture that the Gospel can draw near to mankind, who is the beginning, middle and end of the culture. *"Culture makes the person and the person makes culture."*[182]

Between Christianity and culture there is an unbreakable harmonic connection as there has always been between religion and culture. In order for the Gospel to draw close to culture, and through it to individuals, the Gospel must know the language and intellectual categories of the culture that it meets, its ways of life, its values. That way, it will be able to integrate them into the Christian faith and transform them little by little until the Gospel

---

[181] RH 14

[182] St. John Paul II at the University of Coimbra, Portugal.

becomes a living incarnation in that culture. Inculturation is thus the process by which faith becomes culture.

In such a process, fidelity to the historical experience of God in the context of a particular culture is indispensable, as is fidelity to the apostolic tradition and fidelity to universal ecclesial communion. Inculturation can never be reduced to just one or two of the elements of this threefold fidelity. Regrettably, because of a lack of clarity on this point there have been instances of forced conversion or of superficial adaptations, whose negative results were lamented by Blessed Paul VI in *Evangelii Nuntiandi*.[183] Gospel preaching that is rigid, no-choice, and skin-deep, never produces local churches that are able to transform their sociocultural surroundings or to be missionary. Rather, it has produced a Christianization that is superficial or that has led to various kinds of syncretism.

In its desire to promote authentic evangelization from a healthy inculturation of the Gospel in a plurality of cultures, the Church faces the challenge of finding, in a wise and creative way, new tools and structures for understanding reality, for intercultural dialogue, for theological reflection and formation, and for collegial communion in order to protect and undertake each one of the goals of its activity.

Salvation must reach all humanity and everything that is human in our daily and concrete reality. Through men and women, the Gospel, when it enters into contact with a culture, incorporates that culture's authentic values and ends up creating culture: "Faith that does not become culture is a faith that is not fully embraced, not fully thought through, not faithfully lived," St. John Paul II said in Rome in 1988. Faith makes individuals part of the people of God,

---

[183] EN 20

and it must do so without uprooting them from their own people and culture. Everything the Church does is meant to welcome into its arms those who want to be disciples of Jesus Christ, and it must accompany them day by day on the road of life with all the cultural background that they bring to their life in the community. There is a constant reciprocity between the evangelization of a people and inculturation of the Gospel; but for this reciprocity to be fruitful, it is essential that a culture be capable of expressing the signs of the faith openly and be willing to begin a process of purifying the traditions and folkways that are incompatible with the Gospel. For its part, the Church, must make itself capable of assimilating the values of the people and of understanding how the Gospel is seen from their perspective. In this appropriate balance (which does not mean that there will be no tensions) it will be possible to communicate the Gospel message to a people with all the authenticity and power of the Word of God, but also with all the authenticity and power of the cultural reality and the very essence of the people.

Another important moment in the evolution of this thinking occurred in the Santo Domingo Conference. Its theme was "New Evangelization, Human-Cultural-Christian Promotion." The third chapter of the second part of the *Santo Domingo Document* deals with the theme of Christian culture and offers a full discussion of inculturation[184] and inculturated evangelization.[185] The crisis of the disappearance of human and Christian values is seen as alarming, and a way to respond to this crisis is the inculturation of the Gospel in the light of the three great mysteries of salvation: Christmas (Incarnation), Easter (redemptive suffering) and

---

[184] SDD 230

[185] SDD 248

Pentecost (action of the Spirit, who enables all to understand God's wondrous deeds in their own languages). An inculturated evangelization must be offered to our indigenous brothers and sisters, respecting their cultural expressions and becoming familiar with their world vision, which, starting from a God-man-world universe, creates a unity that suffuses all human, spiritual and transcendent relations. Their symbols, rites and religious expressions that are compatible with the true meaning of the faith are to be valued.[186] In this overall context, the document confirms that today's culture[187] and the city needs a new pastoral strategy.[188]

In the 1990 Encyclical *Redemptoris Missio* St. John Paul II pointed out that with the approach of the third millennium, it was ever more urgent to take the Gospel to all peoples. In the scarcely twenty-five years between the close of the Second Vatican Council (with its missionary Decree *Ad Gentes*) and *Redemptoris Missio*, the number of those who did not know Christ had almost doubled. In his 1994 Post-Synodal Apostolic Exhortation *Ecclesia in Africa*, the Pope wrote that the elements of mission[189] are the following: the witness of Christian life; the *kerygma*, or proclamation, of Christ crucified, dead and risen; conversion and baptism; the formation of Christian communities; inculturation, the process of insertion into the cultures of peoples;[190] dialogue with other religions, and the formation of consciences to promote development— each element to be motivated by love.

---

[186] SDD 248

[187] SDD 252-254

[188] SDD 255ff

[189] That is, the elements of Evangelization and of the New Evangelization. (Trans. note)

[190] SDD 52-54

Inculturation is the inner transformation of cultural values into Christian values, integrating them into the very vision of life, and at the same time, through reflection and praxis, rooting Christianity into the various cultures. It is not an easy process, because the characteristics and the totality of the Christian message must in no way be diluted. To inculturate is to incarnate the Gospel in different cultures, transmit Christian values, and recognize the values held by different cultures, purifying them and avoiding syncretism. This requires periods of preparation and of prudential care, but above all, of wise listening to the voices of the universal Church, of the whole Christian people. It is through reflection and the experience of the Christian people that one arrives at the true meaning of the faith, advances in a genuine sense of faith. Pastors, religious, and the lay faithful, all the people of God, take part in this effort.[191]

For that reason, inculturation of faith or evangelization of culture is framed within the logic of the mystery of the Incarnation, death and resurrection. Inculturation begins with an effort to express faith in the categories and ways of a particular culture, to make it a living reality. In the second step, the Gospel exercises discernment about that culture in order to strip it of all that is in contradiction with the Gospel. From the death of noncompatible, and therefore non-assimilable, elements a new original Christian culture is born. Since every culture is created by human beings, and is therefore marked by sin, every culture must be purified, elevated, and perfected.[192]

In 1994, in the Apostolic Letter *Tertio Millennio Adveniente*, St. John Paul II announced two continental Synods: one for the

---

[191] LG 12

[192] RM 54

Americas, which are unique by reason of their history and social situation, and another for Asia, which is where Christianity meets the most ancient of cultures and local religions.[193]

The Church exists to preach the Gospel,[194] and the goal of evangelization is the inner transformation and renewal of humanity itself. Inculturation is seen as a priority and a condition for evangelization, a path to full evangelization, the great challenge on the eve of the third millennium.[195] Inculturation prepares men and women to receive Jesus Christ in the fullness of their personal, cultural, political and economic beings sanctified through the action of the Holy Spirit.[196] Inculturation is not simply an adaptation of the *kerygma* or of the liturgy, or a tactic to make Christianity attractive at the cost of mutilating Revelation. It is a patient catechesis and a loving search for those "seeds of the Word" which, when they mature, produce the fruits of a civilization of love. It encompasses all areas of the life of the Church—theology, liturgy, and the life and structure of the Church—in its twofold task: that of transforming authentic cultural values and integrating them into Christianity, and that of rooting Christianity in the various human cultures it encounters.[197]

An important aspect of inculturated evangelization is discovering the person, that is, discovering human dignity restored. Through the Incarnation of His only Son, God gives the individual back his or her inalienable dignity as a person and as a child of God. This ministry of social evangelization, which denounces and

---

[193] TMA 38

[194] EN 14

[195] EAf 59

[196] EAf 62

[197] RM 52

combats all that debases and destroys the person, is one part of the inculturation of the Gospel.[198]

Inculturation as Action of the Holy Spirit

"Through inculturation the Church makes the Gospel incarnate in varying cultures and at the same time introduces peoples, together with their individual cultures, into her own community. She transmits to them her own values, at the same time taking the good elements that already exist in them and renewing them from within."[199]

"Inculturation is a movement towards full evangelization. It seeks to dispose people to receive Jesus Christ in an integral manner. It touches them on the personal, cultural, economic and political levels so that they can live a holy life in total union with God the Father, through the action of the Holy Spirit."[200]

To penetrate and to ferment with the yeast of the Gospel the ways of thinking, feeling and acting of cultures not our own, the action of the Holy Spirit is necessary and indispensable. He is the one who animates history and can lead it to the "new creation."[201]

This Spirit is the one present at the Incarnation, and in the life, death and resurrection of Jesus, and acting in the Church. All that the Spirit works in individuals and in the history of peoples is preparation for the Gospel and cannot but refer to Christ, the Word incarnate by the power of the Holy Spirit "in order, as perfect man, to save all and renew all things."[202]

---

[198] EAf 70

[199] RM 52

[200] EAf 62

[201] Rev. 21:5

[202] RM 29

Inculturation is also closely bound to the mystery of Pentecost, thanks to the outpouring and action of the Spirit, who unifies gifts and talents. All peoples of the Earth, on joining the Church, live a new Pentecost, profess in their own language the one faith in Jesus Christ, and proclaim the wondrous works that the Lord has accomplished in them. The Spirit, who is the source of the wisdom of peoples, guides the Church with a supernatural light toward knowledge of all truth. In turn, the Church, taking up the values of the different cultures, becomes *"sponsa ornata monilibus suis"* ("a bride adorned with her jewels").[203]

What happened that day was certainly mysterious but was also significant. In Pentecost we can see a sign of the universality of Christianity and of the missionary character of the Church. The author of Acts presents the Church to us knowing that the message is destined for people of "all nations," and that, in addition, it is the Holy Spirit who intervenes so that all can understand at least something in their own language: "We hear them speaking in our own native tongue."[204] Today we would speak of an adaptation to the linguistic and cultural conditions of each person. Therefore, one can see all of this as an early form of "inculturation," accomplished through the power of the Holy Spirit.[205]

God's revelation cannot but be inculturated, although cultures differ and change, as do individuals, throughout history. That is why the Good News will live only through the power of the Spirit, who makes the Word of God resound with saving power, who makes it challenging, and who causes it to be proclaimed in a way that enables all to embrace it in the circumstances in which they

---

[203] Is. 61:10, EAf 61

[204] Acts 2:8

[205] General Audience, Wednesday, Sept. 20, 1989.

100

live. It is the Spirit whose help ensures respect for all the various expressions of faith. Through the action of the Spirit, God's communication of Himself remains clear in changing circumstances. Naturally, the various transcultural expressions of the Gospel message progressively enrich our understanding of it. In addition, our knowledge of the revealed, transmitted and experienced mystery increases, with the Spirit leading us to full truth.

Inculturation and Traditional Piety

Inculturation of faith is one of the most important issues in the Church today. The synthesis between culture and faith is needful for both culture and faith. "A faith that does not become culture is a faith not fully embraced, not totally thought out, nor faithfully lived"[206] Faith is not an idea, not a philosophy, not an ideology. Faith proceeds from a personal encounter with Jesus Christ, the Son of God made flesh. Once a person discovers the love of God in his or her life, he or she is not the same as before. A people who believes in the living and true God, Jesus Christ, and follows Him, is a special people. For them, traditional piety is the faith of the simple people, the faith that becomes life and culture. It is the special way a people has of living and expressing their relationship with God, with our Lady, and with the saints in a private and intimate atmosphere, but also, and especially, in the community.

In order to evaluate traditional piety positively, we have to start from a radically hopeful anthropology. The person has to be defined by his openness to transcendence. We must begin with an anthropology that considers the person as a unity of body and

---

[206] St. John Paul II, Letter with which he instituted the Pontifical Council for Culture, May 20, 1982.

101

spirit, open to the infinite. The person discovers God by examining what he himself is, and does, in the concrete reality of his life. The God of Christian revelation manifests Himself in these activities, opening them to their transcendent destinies.

At the Puebla Conference there was discussion of anthropologies that are unacceptable because they are not compatible with the religious dimension of the person: anthropologies based on such things as determinism, psychology, economics, statism, and science.

Appreciation of traditional piety starts from a conception of the person as a transcendent and sacred being. Humans are the only creatures able to adore, and human beings show their intelligence when they arrive at an adoring profession of faith. Christian anthropology begins by presupposing the dignity of the person and of all his manifestations, among which are found all the expressions of traditional piety.

Traditional piety is simply the piety of a believing people who cannot but express publically, with sincere and simple spontaneity, their Christian faith, passed down from generation to generation, shaping the life and customs of a whole people.

Appreciating its historical identity and returning to its roots, the Catholic Church in Latin America, especially since the Second Vatican Council, has rediscovered in a positive way the piety that has flourished within it since its beginnings in the sixteenth century.

But it is not only the vigor of traditional piety in the life of the peoples of Latin America that has obligated intellectuals to reevaluate that piety; it has also been the history of traditional piety, which has shown itself to be a veritable treasure house for the cultural synthesis that created Latin America in the sixteenth and seventeenth centuries, a jealous custodian of the variety of interconnections linking its Indian, African and European origins.

Recognizing the true value of traditional piety means recognizing the true value of the Church's past and of its historical continuity among Latin Americans.

From this perspective, traditional piety can be considered as one of the few instances of the cultural synthesis in Latin America that runs throughout all eras of its history and that embraces at the same time all of its dimensions: work and production, the location of settlements, lifestyles, language and the arts, political organization, and daily life. Precisely in its role as the treasure house of cultural identity, traditional piety has withstood the efforts of modernity to subordinate individual cultures to the dictates of reason.

Traditional piety has been present in Catholicism from its beginnings. In Latin America, the doctrine that missionaries brought was combined with African or indigenous practices, resulting, in some instances, in combined, very well-integrated ceremonies.

With the passage of time and with migration to urban areas, the traditional piety of the countryside spread to the cities.

The flourishing of different expressions of traditional piety in great urban areas is a response to individuals' need to recover their socioreligious roots, their natural openness to the transcendent, and their spiritual values. In the face of modernization and, even more, of postmodernity, it has been a communitary form of resistance, a "prophetic cry" from individuals who do not want to deny mystery and the transcendent in their lives. People from the countryside who become city-dwellers feel uprooted from their land and traditions and thrown into a world in which only personal gain and specialized training counts. Their natural tendency would be to go back where they came from, but not being really able to, they take refuge in what symbolizes their essence, their land, their traditions. In this way, urban traditional piety emerges and provides a bridge to make an apparently impossible connection. With traditional piety, and all its emotional components, they reconnect with their most intimate being, even if their living conditions do not change. With saints, devotions and fiestas, they find themselves among their own and with what identifies them most deeply, and thus are able to make their unwelcoming surroundings into a home.

Traditional piety, as a visible and profound manifestation of the religious sentiment of a people, is an example of incarnation of the faith within cultural realities, which it permeates while at the same time being enriched by them; that is to say, traditional piety is an example of inculturation of the faith. It is deeply felt, emotional; it is not abstract or rational. It is expressed in varied types of devotional practices through which, by means of symbols, the religious and specifically Christian values connected to differing cultural universes are lived out, thus making traditional piety a form of self-evangelization. We can truly understand traditional piety only if we recognize that culture is an interrelated whole.

The experience of the faith that is identified with traditional piety springs from the very heart of human experience and is bound up with symbols, stories, myths, beliefs, dreams. "More than to word and analysis, it gives precedence to action, ceremony, myth, movement, embraces, song, music, eloquent silences, dances, candles, flowers and so forth."[207]

The *Puebla Document* sees in Latin American traditional piety a *"wise manifestation that integrates culture and faith: It is a treasury of values that reflect Christian wisdom; it is the wisdom of the Catholic people; it assimilates creatively the divine and the human; it is a Christian humanism that radically affirms the dignity of every person as a child of God; it establishes fundamental brotherhood; it teaches how to encounter nature and how to understand work, and it gives a reason for joy and humor, even in the midst of life's great difficulties. For the people, it is an evangelical principle, and instinct, for discernment."[208]*

Traditional piety reflects a deep sense of transcendence and, at the same time, a real experience of the nearness of God. It can express the faith in coherent language that overcomes rationalistic attitudes through contemplation that defines a person's relationship with nature and with others. It gives meaning to work, to fiestas, to solidarity, to friendship, to the family; and it gives a feeling of contentment with one's own dignity—dignity not diminished by the poverty and simplicity of individual lives.

Traditional piety is heartfelt. Faith is ruled by sentiment. Even if some do not accept this kind of religion, arguing that it does entail personal commitment, nevertheless the sentiments of the heart enable faith to express itself in thoughtful gestures and kindnesses toward the Lord and toward one's brethren. Sensitivity is not incompatible with deep spiritual experiences. As proof, all

---

[207] Argentinian Archbishop Víctor Manuel Fernández (b. 1962), Rector of the Pontifical Catholic University of Argentina in Buenos Aires, *Una interpretación de la religiosidad popular. Criterio,* 2300 (Dec. 2004).

[208] PD 448

we have to do is look to the great mystics of the Catholic Church, such as St. John of the Cross, St. Teresa or St. Ignatius of Loyola, who show us the sensitive side of faith. In a healthy and enriching interchange, traditional piety contributes to the Church, which is often tempted to intellectualize and concentrate only on ideas and formulations that do not inspire radical commitment.

These expressions of traditional piety are *"the sign that the faith has taken root in the hearts of peoples and entered into their daily lives. In this sense, traditional piety is the first and fundamental form of inculturation of the faith."*[209] *"Faith that has become culture is lived spontaneously, as an inseparable part of one's life, and therefore it is more than a series of ideas: Faith becomes fertile and heartfelt; it configures a particular way of living and of expressing the power of the Spirit. Inculturated faith is not just mass religious gatherings; it is also those religious acts that gradually come to be part of everyday life, of our spontaneous and familiar language, and that most people feel to be part of their identity. It is what a person has in common with other believers but is also, at the same time, very personal."*[210]

The experience of faith manifested in daily gestures and lived in a community leads to the love of God and neighbor, and helps individuals and peoples become aware of their responsibility in the creation of history and in the fulfillment of their own destinies. Traditional piety is made up of a series of very important human and religious values: *"It manifests a thirst for God that only the simple and poor can know. It renders individuals capable of generosity and sacrifice, even to the point of heroism, when they*

---

[209] Archbishop Víctor Manuel Fernández, *Hundir mi camino en esta tierra. Y quedarme: La incarnación terrena de la espiritualidad pastoral. Vida Pastoral,* 238 (2002).

[210] *Directorio sobre la piedad popular y la liturgia,* 91 (2002)

are called on to stand up for what they believe. It involves an acute awareness of the attributes of God: fatherhood, providence, loving and constant presence. It engenders interior attitudes rarely observed to the same degree elsewhere: patience, the sense of the Cross in daily life, detachment, openness to others, devotion.[211] From an anthropological perspective, traditional piety manifests deep sentiments that are "there from the dawn," as Mircea Eliade[212] might have put it: closeness to nature, contact with life and death, the need to feel safe and to feel oneself a part of a complex reality. This attitude of individuals demonstrates, at one and the same time, the need for safety amid threats to existence and the need to give unity to life with symbols and stories.

In Latin America, traditional piety gives form to historical identity: It is a history of evangelization that integrates, more or less consciously, a multitude of cultural and religious elements from many peoples, races, and cultures. Underlying traditional piety are indigenous contributions (such as rhythms, clothing, music, food), African-Amerindian culture affected by the experience of slavery, nostalgia for the homeland expressed in trance and healing ceremonies, contributions from rural areas, and the influence of the marginalized urban social strata that band together to maintain their values.

From all this comes "the importance of traditional piety for the life of faith of the people of God, for the preservation of that faith itself. Traditional piety has been a providential instrument for the preservation of faith where Christians lacked pastoral care."[213] In

---

[211] EN 48

[212] Romanian historian of religion, philosopher, essayist, novelist, linguist (1907-1986). (Trans. note)

[213] *Directorio sobre la piedad popular y la liturgia, passim.*

this sense, we must emphasize the importance of the Christian signs that permeate popular culture, creating in millions of individuals a favorable attitude towards God and resulting in a spontaneous transmission of Christian spirituality. The touching piety of the poor has often become a path used by the Spirit to reach hearts and to begin the return to a life of friendship with God by many who had fallen away. In other cases, it has sustained a silent but intense devotion to the faith by providing a sense of identity and belonging.

In this transmission the people are not an anonymous, passive grouping; they are active participants. For a long time the majority of the poor were not accepted as cultural actors. For this reason, and because of ingrained prejudice against the common people, Latin American religion was considered archaic, fetishistic and fit only for the ignorant. *"In the most authentic manifestations of traditional piety, in fact, the Christian message on the one hand assimilates the modes of expression of the culture of the people, and on the other infuses the Gospel teaching about life and death, freedom, liberty, mission and the destiny of humanity into the people's thinking. In that way, the transmission of culture from parents to children, from one generation to another, brings the transmission of Christian principles with it. In some cases the union of culture and faith is so strong that elements proper to the Christian faith have been converted into components of the cultural identity of a people. Devotion to the Mother of God is one example of this phenomenon."*[214] The *Aparecida Document* even refers to traditional piety as "the people's mysticism."[215]

---

[214] *Directorio sobre la piedad popular y la liturgia*, 63.

[215] AD 216

The Church is facing a variety of challenges. Today more than ever, when an evangelization project is proposed, the question of life is raised. Clearly, the whole Church is aware that what is at stake is "life" and, as a consequence, the "abundant life" that Jesus Christ brings. Hence the need to focus all our efforts on that situation. The *Aparecida Document* puts before our eyes the reality of the culture of death, the most evident signs of which are increased poverty—even extreme poverty—concentration of wealth, inequality, the law of the market, economic neoliberalism, tax havens, the crisis of democracy, corruption, migration, discrimination, terrorism, environmental pollution, the crisis of the family, abortion, euthanasia, subjectivism, consumerism, the imposition of modern culture (with its contempt for ancestral cultures), individualism, the crisis of values, moral relativism, and the disappearance of faith from daily life.

It is hard for the Church to accept that after having inspired Latin American life and culture for more than five centuries, the religious consciousness of the people has eroded.[216] Faith is not transmitted from generation to generation with the same ease as in the past.[217] The *Aparecida Document*, rather than bemoaning or condemning the situation, humbly recognizes that it does not have the answers for all the problems and that the situation is an invitation to the Church to discern reality in the light of the Holy Spirit, to place itself at the service of the Kingdom in that reality.[218]

It is indispensable for us to be *"consumed by missionary zeal, to bring to the heart of the culture of our time that unifying and full meaning of human life that neither science, nor politics, nor*

---

[216] AD 38

[217] AD 39

[218] AD 33

economics, nor the media can provide. In Christ the Word, God's Wisdom,[219] *culture can again find its center and depth, from which to view reality in all its aspects, discerning them in the light of the Gospel and granting to each its place and proper dimension."*[220] Missionary disciples are called to be creative in the areas of culture, politics, public opinion, art and science— areas that have frequently been ignored—"taking on with new energy the option for the poor."[221] "The evangelization of culture, far from abandoning the preferential option for the poor, renews it."[222] The commitment to this reality is born from passionate love for Christ, who, with His ardent and tireless Samaritan charity, accompanies the people of God in their mission to inculturate the Gospel in history.

The Church, in order to take up the great work of the Kingdom as Jesus did, will renew its ways of drawing close to others, of relating and interacting, as well as rediscovering anchor points within existing cultures.

Evangelization of the present-day postmodern culture is crying out for a pastoral effort, both within and outside the Church, that takes into account language, actions, signs and symbols—a vision that expresses a commitment to the truth about God and about humanity.

This implies the creation of a new cultural paradigm as a true alternative to the now-dominant way of thinking, a paradigm that takes into account the major concerns and interests of people today: social reality, ecological thinking, modern cosmology, ethnicities, peace, the ethics of care, mercy and compassion.

---

[219] 1 Cor. 1:30

[220] AD 41

[221] AD 399

[222] AD 397-9

Traditional Piety as Inculturation of the Faith

Drawing on the most important statements about it in the *Aparecida Document*, traditional piety is a privileged pathway in this quest for a new paradigm. It is, for the Latin American peoples, an expression of Catholic faith; it contains the most valuable dimension of Latin American culture; it delicately permeates the personal existence of each believer, but it is also alive in a crowd; its depths can be plumbed and it can continually permeate more deeply the way of life of our peoples. It is a necessary starting point for the maturation and increased fruitfulness of the faith of people to mature and become more fruitful. It contains and expresses an intense sense of the transcendent, a spontaneous capacity to rely on God, and a true experience of theological love; it is a legitimate way to live the faith, an expression of supernatural wisdom, a means of feeling part of the Church, and a way of being missionary; it is a powerful confession of the living God who acts in history, and it is a channel for the transmission of the faith.[223]

Religion, through its various lively and meaningful expressions, can come to the rescue of the person, of his or her identity and vocation. In the words of Pope Emeritus Benedict XVI, "The soul of the Latin American peoples is found in their piety"; it is "the precious treasure of the Catholic Church in Latin America" and "it reflects a thirst for God that only the poor and the simple can know." Ordinary people have created and transmitted, over many centuries, the manifestations of traditional piety that are the ways in which they celebrate life.

---

[223] AD 258-259, 261-264

Shrines

Throughout all of Latin America and the Caribbean are beloved spaces for particular expressions of traditional piety. The places, shrines, have a prominent place in the history of the Christian faith in these lands. Without the presence and pastoral activity of the shrines, it would be very difficult for the Church to be connected with the many groups of peoples who, even though they do not always express it in formal ways, identify with the Catholic faith. In their piety, ordinary people turn to these shrines and remember that their origin is in the Lord, and also that the God who loved us once never stops loving us; that today, in the very moment in history in which we find ourselves faced with the contradictions and the sufferings of the present, God travels with us on the road of life.

Just as the Old and New Testaments witness with one voice that the Temple is the place for remembering salvation history and for experiencing present grace, the shrine is the sign of divine presence, the place of making ever new the covenant that humanity has entered into with the Eternal and with itself. By going to the Temple, the pious Israelite rediscovered the faithfulness of the God of the promise in each "today" of history. The Temple is the holy abode of the Ark of the Covenant, the place where the pact with the living God is realized and the people of God are aware that they are building a community of believers, the "chosen people, royal priesthood, holy nation."[224]

The shrine is the place of the Spirit because it is the place where the fidelity of God reaches the individual and transforms him or her. Above all, one goes to the shrine to invoke and embrace the grace of the Spirit, and to take it afterward to all of life's activities. The shrine is, par excellence, the place of the Word,

---

[224] 1 Peter 2:9

the privileged place of forgiveness, reconciliation and thanksgiving. In it, the faithful, through the sacraments, bring about an encounter with Him who, in consolation and hope, continually nourishes with new life all who come to Him hungry and thirsty. Pilgrims go to the shrines as if to the temple of the living God, the place of the living covenant with Him, so that the grace of the Sacraments can free them from sin and give them new enthusiasm, joy and strength to be clear witnesses to the Eternal among men. This renewed fidelity of God gives rise to covenants that are expressed in the vows pilgrims make.

At the shrine, one learns to open one's heart to all, in particular to those who are different from us: the visitor, the stranger, the immigrant, the refugee, the one who professes another religion, and the nonbeliever. In this way, the shrine, in addition to being a place to experience Church, becomes an open gathering place for all humanity. *"The experience of shrine piety constitutes a special way of approaching ordinary people, who are so often distant from the more common forms of pastoral activity. Pilgrimage becomes a chance to communicate the Gospel—expressed, lived and contextualized in the symbolism and rhythms that are part of the lives of the faithful."*[225]

Pilgrimage

Pilgrimages are another expression of traditional piety connected to the shrines. They are a profound symbolic expression that manifests deeply the human search for meaning, for a real encounter with "the other," and for what transcends us and is beyond all possibility, difference and time. Pilgrimage allows the

---

[225] *Final Declaration of the Fourth Congress of Rectors of Shrines in Latin America and the Caribbean.*

experience of searching and of openness to be shared in traveling with other pilgrims and to reach our hearts, giving rise to sentiments of deep solidarity.

Fiestas

Fiestas occupy another important place in traditional piety. They embody closure, fulfillment, and joyful gratitude with singing and dancing. Fiestas involve all the senses in an atmosphere of satisfaction and joy. Time is measured by a different rhythm of concentrated activity and rest, of religious ceremonies and secular activities. It is not a show with an audience and actors. Onlookers become participants. The presence of outsiders, even complete strangers, intensifies awareness of what is being celebrated, for the revelers feel an obligation to explain what they are celebrating. In addition, fiestas give identity to a people because the celebration brings neighbors together, welcomes back those who have emigrated, and attracts newcomers.

Marian Devotion

Strongly rooted in the faith of our people, Marian devotion is one of the principal indicators of Latin American identity, as the alliance with Yahweh was for Israel. Israel knew it was the chosen people, the custodian of the law and the prophets. By reason of its relationship with a God who was near, Israel was aware of its own uniqueness. By analogy, the Christian people understands that the protection of God comes to them through prayers before a personalized and unique image of Mary, and that therefore Mary embodies that people and makes it unique.

The people feel identified with the image of Mary because their parents had recourse to her, and today they go with their own problems. Admiring the personal virtues of Mary, traditional piety takes advantage of her influence to get to God. Mary's miraculous actions are the principal sign of individualized protection over a place, and from a place. Pleas and petitions for favors are a manifestation of the mother-child covenant, of personal relationships, of mutual commitment. Even if they rarely approach the Sacraments, people react to sickness and suffering by making a vow. They might promise to go to the shrine on foot; to go on the journey in silence; to circle the chapel on their knees, with arms outstretched; to bring candles or a donation; but most of the vows are private, and the reasons for them stay with the person or the family.

The law of incarnation can be felt in the traditional manifestations of Marian piety. Inculturation of the faith doesn't mean that the faith is just poured into already existing cultural molds. Faith creates its own signs of identity and its own molds for living together in society. It makes them known; it fills them with life, and it communicates life. In the words of the theologian Lucio Gera,[226] *"The People is like water. Its path is like the course of rivers, which inevitably meander. Sometimes, like mountain streams that flow impetuously and turbulent straight into the valley. Sometimes, like our rivers of the pampas that are calm,*

---

[226] *The people is like water.* (COMITÉ TEOLÓGICO EDITORIAL, *Escritos teológicos pastorales de Lucio Gera, II. De la Conferencia de Puebla a nuestros días* (1982-2007), Buenos Aires 2007, 920-921). (1924-2012) Considered by many to be the most important Argentinian theologian of the second half of the twentieth century, Lucio Gera (1924-2012) was the most well-known exponent of the "Theology of the People," a non-Marxist current, originating in Argentina, of liberation theology. It gave special importance to inculturation and traditional piety. See the following link:
http://www.americalatina.va/content/americalatina/es/secciones/articulos---reflexiones/otros/lucio-gera--in-memoriam--16-1-1924--7-8-2012--.html
(Trans. note)

peaceful and 'aimless' and that after playful wanderings flow into the ocean. Sometimes, finally, like our Paraná, that flows past San Nicolás and that when it is low, looks calm but hides within itself the unexpected force of a torrent. The People is like water in rivers, which are pilgrims heading for the ocean. Because they are pilgrims and not simply wanderers, rivers have their own direction and goal. Coming from the mountain, they go to the sea; coming from Above, they go towards Infinity. Being a river, being a People, consists precisely in knowing of a common origin, and having a feeling that there is a common destiny. And this conviction is strengthened in peoples when, like drops of water, in their Christian faith they are mixed with the blood of Christ. Because blood— that is, life, Christ's life, and in Christ ours— also comes from a Place and passing through death arrives at Resurrection. This is the faith of our People. But a People, the believing People that is a pilgrim on this Earth, that is water and blood, is always a torrent. A river in torrent, a torrent of blood. A torrent that boasts of its vitality, in the energy with which it seeks truth, in the power of its love and in the power that its ideals give it. All these forces converge again and again in passion and imagination.

"The torrent is the imagination of the people that draws with it everything that it finds and that it invents, mixing them randomly. Imagination is invention. The imagination of the people is not only the ability to make up stories, it is also the ability to see truths. The truths that are behind the stories, the anecdotes, the legends, meaningful cores of truth adorned with flamboyant decorations by the same playful habit of the imagination. Birth and death, man meeting woman, love and loneliness, work and sickness, doing good and introducing evil: all ask the question about truth that surrounds the enigma and mystery of life. Trying to give answers in the form of divinatory intuitions. From the moment that it

enfolds within itself something divine, life becomes a riddle. Desperately seeking truth, the People gropes for it, imagines it. This desire makes it easier to accept the word of truth that God reveals in Christ. But at the same time, the People will continue to give free rein to its imagination as it circles around revealed truth."

The proposal of the *Aparecida Document* is a call to live this moment in our history as a saving and ecclesial event. In this light, the mission of the Church is presented as a tireless effort to unite the transcendent and the immanent, the eternal and the day-to-day, in a single message; and in this effort, traditional piety, as a certain and tangible expression of the faith born under the shadow of many sufferings, has much to tell us. To quote Ernesto Sábato, "The greatest nobility is to carry out one's work in the midst of devastation, supporting it tirelessly, halfway between heartbreak and beauty."[227] In each moment in history, from the Old Testament until today, when we have felt a sense of total failure and downfall, we have saved ourselves thanks to the most defenseless part of humanity. The mission of the Church presents itself as a service to a full, dignified and joyous life in Christ and cannot leave aside the poor and simple people who, amidst the difficulties of their everyday lives, give flesh to this mission.

As God's pilgrim people in Latin America and the Caribbean, we, as missionary disciples, entrust ourselves to the tenderness, beauty and joy of God's love manifested in the mestizo face of the Mother of God, the Virgin of Guadalupe. She holds her people in the apple of her eye, and shelters it in the folds of her mantle. Her hands folded in prayer encourage us to cast our nets to bring

---

[227] *Before the End. Memoirs,* 1998. Ernesto Roque Sábato (1911-2011) was a major literary and intellectual figure in twentieth-century Argentina.

everyone close to Jesus, "the Way, the Truth, and the Light,"[228] because He wants all to "have life and have it to the full."[229]

---

[228] Jn. 14:6
[229] Jn. 10:10

CHAPTER SIX
EDUCATION AND ENCOUNTER[230]

At Harvard University, in Cambridge, Massachusetts, in the United States, the following Scripture quote is engraved on the façade of one of its buildings: "What is man that Thou art mindful of him?"[231] A magnificent question that has to guide anyone who wants to think about education. As we do today.

What is communicated in that question, full of wonderment, taken from the eighth Psalm, is not surprise that God is interacting directly with humanity—He often does in the Old Testament—it is1 rather the *quality* of that interaction, *mindfulness*, the constant showering of divine attention that the Scriptures express in a single word, "love."

After the surprise, after the impact produced by the actions of the Creator in favor of His most beloved work, another question arises, the metaphysical question: What is the nature of the beneficiary of so much care?

"What is man?" "What are we?"

In this context, the biblical phrase allows for two ways of understanding the mystery of humanity: a theological approach, or else a philosophical, cultural, scientific approach—an upward path from works that are seen, to arrive at the very center from which those works proceed.

---

[230] Speech to the Christian Association of Businessmen on the subject of education, September 1, 1999.

[231] Ps. 8:4. The inscription is over the main entrance to the Philosophy Department building, Emerson Hall, named after Harvard alumnus and American author and lecturer Ralph Waldo Emerson (1803-1882). See http://www.waymarking.com/waymarks/WM8AZ9_Emerson_Hall_Harvard_Un iversity_Cambridge_MA (Trans. note)

The first way guides us—without our being any less struck than the Psalmist—toward God's educational plan for humanity, in which He speaks His Word to us; and that Word becomes so close and present to us in history that it becomes one of us: Jesus Christ. To mankind, Christ fully reveals mankind itself, and mankind's dignity.

The Psalmist's question is relevant because men and women need somehow to know what they are so they can *learn to be* what they are. Their nature, their essence, are givens; but they must accomplish themselves, become themselves. And this process of humanization is what we call education.

Men and women activate their potential, and in doing so become themselves and produce a culture. The subject of a culture is a community, a people, which creates for itself a way of living. Education is all about passing on that culture.

Men and women, and entire peoples, express themselves with what they produce, but we must add that we are also *that which we are working to be*. Thus, we can be defined by our aspirations as well as by our accomplishments.

At the end of the millennium, we talk about a crisis of culture, a crisis of values. All this touches the core of each human being, as a person and as a member of society.

We worry about what is happening. We must not forget that evil breaks in and takes over only where it finds a void in the human spirit, so our careful judgment is called for.

Discerning Culture

In our globalized culture, pieces of what some call the "flotsam and jetsam of a shipwrecked culture" wash up on our shores, relics of modernism, which is disappearing, and of its successor, postmodernism, which is gaining ground.

Let me attempt to point out and explain some of postmodernism's features.

a) Profane Messianism. This appears in various forms of social and political undertakings. Sometimes it shifts the ethos of personal actions to structures, with the result that instead of ethos creating structures, structures create ethos. That is why its path to sociopolitical salvation is to concentrate on the "analysis of structures" and of the sociopolitical initiatives that spring from them. Underlying this attitude is the belief that ethos is a fragile element whereas structures are a value that is solid and safe. All of this involves a tension between action and structure. Ethos is thought to be incapable of supporting a proper tension between action and structure (what arises from personal interiority is considered "action"), and tends to move toward structures since they are naturally more stable and of greater weight. When the personal sense of a goal (the common good, God) is lost, all that remains is the power of "quantity," which is what defines structures.

b) Relativism. The present tendency to discredit values or—at least to favor an immanent moralism that ignores the transcendent, replacing it with false promises or contingent goals—is the fruit of uncertainty, contaminated by mediocrity. When values are separated from their Christian roots, they become monads, commonplaces, or no more than labels.

Relativism is the possibility of fantasizing about reality, of thinking about it as if it could be controlled like a game. Relativism forces us to evaluate and to judge based only on our subjective impressions; it has no practical, concrete or objective norms.

In relativism, ethics and politics are reduced to physics. Neither good nor evil exists *in itself*; they are only the sum of advantages and disadvantages. Departure from right reason[232] has as its consequence the fact that law cannot be based on a fundamental idea of justice; it becomes instead the reflection of dominant ideas. This subjectivist retreat from values leads us to take action based on uncertain consensus. And here things get worse: Civilization goes downhill because it relies on negotiated consensus, and in those circumstances force always wins.

With relativism, opinion rules. There are no certainties, no convictions. Everything is acceptable. But it is a very short walk from everything being acceptable to nothing mattering any more.

c) Autonomy. Men and women today are *rootless* and *abandoned.* They got that way from the excessive desire for autonomy that they inherited from modernism. They no longer rely on anything transcendent.

d) Nihilism. There is a new nihilism that universalizes everything, nullifying and devaluing the particular—or advancing it with such violence that it is destroyed. Fratricidal conflict, total internationalization of capital and of the media, indifference to concrete sociopolitical commitments and to participation in culture and values: all are the result of this nihilism.

We want the illusion of an individuality that is autonomous and uncategorized, but we end up being a statistic, a target of advertising.

---

[232] In the original Spanish, "*razón moral*" (Trans. Note)

e) Reason. The modern meaning given to *razón* [233] is one-sided: Only "quantitative reasoning" (geometry as perfect science), and the "ratios" used in calculations and experimentation have the right to be called *razón.*

f) Gnosticism. A technologically oriented mind-set, together with the search for profane messianism are two identifying traits of men and women today. We can call them "Gnostics": full of information but all of it disjointed, and—on the other hand— addicted to the esoteric, but to an esoteric that is secularized, profane. We might say that the temptation of education is to be gnostic and esoteric, lacking as it does the internal unity that comes from having real goals and working on a human scale, being thus unable to dominate technology. This situation cannot be overcome by any kind of "return" (of the type that dying modernism stubbornly seeks). Rather, it will be overcome only by letting an "internal information overload" happen, that is, by striking at the very heart of the situation and overcoming it totally, transcending it without being enveloped by it.

g) A false hermeneutic that leads to mistrust. Use is made of fallacy, which is an untruth that fascinates because it seems to be correct. Only slowly do its pernicious effects become evident.

What is true and noble is caricatured by exaggerating some elements with ridicule or cruelty and ignoring many others. It's a way to minimize what is good. Over and over, in public and private, it's easy to make fun of some value or other: honesty,

---

[233] In Spanish, *razón* can mean either "reason" or "ratio." (Trans. note)

nonviolence, modesty. But that only leads to our losing respect for that value, thus strengthening its opposite and cheapening our lives.

Or a slogan is invented that uses rich verbal or visual communication to absolutize one aspect and disfigure the whole.

h) Deism. Postmodernism is no longer opposed to religion, and still less does it force it into the purely private realm. What is accepted is a *watered-down deism,* which reduces faith and religion to spiritualism and subjectivity (which produces a faith without piety). Elsewhere, fundamentalism takes root, but its weaknesses and superficiality are soon revealed.

This pitiful kind of transcendence, which can't admit of any limits to immanence, exists only because on the one hand it is afraid of setting boundaries and on the other it avoids dealing with human suffering.

Closely joined to this deistic model is a process whereby words lose their meaning (words with no weight, words with no meat on them). They're emptied of their content. Christ is no longer a Person. He's an idea. Inflation even affects words. The culture is nominalist. Words have lost their weight; they're empty. They have nothing backing them up; no "spark" that brings them to life, especially if that spark can sometimes be silence.

The Culture of Encounter

Let me offer a proposal: We need to create a culture of encounter.

Faced with a *culture of fragmentation*, as it is sometimes called, or of non-integration, we are called on in these difficult times not to support those who want to capitalize on resentment, on forgetting our shared history, or on weakening the bonds that hold us together.

a) Incarnate realism. We must always let the suffering, defenseless and worried faces we see be the inspiration for our commitment to continued research, study and work. The men and women we meet—they are to be the focus of our mission.

Flesh-and-blood men and women belonging to a definite culture with a definite history, and the complexity of all that is human with its tensions and its limits—none of this is respected today or taken into account. Still, it is humanity that must be at the center of our efforts and our study. The fact that humanity has its limits, that there are concrete and objective laws and norms, that authority is always necessary but always imperfect, and that we must be committed to reality: these are obstacles that the mentality I described above cannot overcome.

Let us run from virtual realities. And run as well from the worship of what only *seems* to be real.

b) Memory. No one who neglects *memory* can educate. Memory is a force that unifies and integrates. Left to its own devices, the intellect runs off a cliff. Likewise, memory is at the very heart of a family and of a people, and a family without memory is unworthy of the name. A family that neither respects nor takes care of its grandparents, who are its living memory, is a family that has come apart. But a family and a people that remembers is a family and a people that has a future.

The key is to not smother the creative force of our own history, our history that has much to tell us. Education, the continuing search for wisdom, is an appropriate place to rediscover the principles that make it possible to fulfill our desires, to fulfill the mission that, while hidden in those desires, strives always to be carried out.

We see so much memory that is weak, fading, nothing but recalled bits and pieces, distracted by "breaking news," fads, passing fancies, and ill-thought-out pronouncements that do no more than cover up ignorance. All these fragments attempt to hide history and deny it.

For example, the legal structure of the City of Buenos Aires was recently modified, but that should not lead us to assume that we are "starting from zero." Only for someone who has no history is nothing ever finished. For that person, all is in the future; everything has to always "start from zero."

c) From cultural escapism to transcendence that can be built on. One has to formulate an anthropology that renounces any possibility of "going back to the way things were," of a more or less conscious quest for a cultural Brigadoon. Out of laziness, individuals tend to rebuild the familiar. This tendency is a consequence of what I said earlier. Modernism—as it loses support—has recourse to what is "classic" (in the sense of the classical world, the ancient world) as an expression of "the way things should be" in a culture. When it finds itself divided, divorced from itself, it confuses its own nostalgia for transcendence with its yearning for direct but sometimes rootless interactions. A rootless and disunited culture cannot stand.

d) Universalism that integrates by respecting differences. We must enter globalized culture starting from a vision of universality. Instead of being atoms that find their meaning only as parts of a whole, we must integrate ourselves into a new, higher, living organic structure that takes on what is ours, but without destroying it. We integrate ourselves harmoniously into something that transcends us, but without giving up what is ours.

And this cannot be done through consensus, which is a downhill path, it must take the path of dialogue, of the exchange of ideas and of the exercise of authority.

e) Dialogue as the most human form of communication. In every environment there must be a place for dialogue that is serious and appropriate, not just a formality or waste of time. It is an exchange that destroys prejudices, builds through joint research, and strives to promote the interaction of wills working in common on shared projects.

Dialogue is even more necessary in times like ours, where we're known as "information's children but communication's orphans." We need patience, clarity and good will toward others. We can have disagreements, divergent points of view, but we must always use ideas to enlighten, not to defeat—as light bulbs, not as weapons. We don't lay aside our ideas, our dreams, our intellectual property or our rights. The only thing we give up is any insistence on their being unique or absolute.

f) The proper exercise of authority. Guidance is always necessary, and that means taking part in the formalities that render a community cohesive; but a guide's role is not to advance his own view—it is to be totally of service. How complete is the degradation of community life that results from policies based on *faits accomplis* that make true participation in society impossible and that value formalities over reality!

Persons who are in authority must have respect for the specific worldviews that give internal structure to all the several areas of education, from the elementary level to postgraduate studies. This respect manifests itself in the honor given to legitimate pluralism and in the freedom to teach and to learn.

So that the strength we all have within ourselves (which make possible human bonds and life) may become visible, it is necessary for all of us—and particularly those who exercise significant political or economic power or any other type of influence—to renounce those special interests and abuses of power that harm the common good that unites us. We must accept with modesty and greatness of spirit the mission that these times impose on us.

g) Creating spaces of encounter. Far removed from superficiality and earthbound arbitrariness (which are blossoms that don't bear fruit), there is a people that has a collective memory and that doesn't fail to move forward with the dignity that is its hallmark. Present-day community efforts and initiatives, the growth of neighborhood undertakings, and the growth of so many mutual assistance movements are a sign of God's presence in a whirlwind of activity, free of special interests (only rarely seen in our country). Our people—who know how to organize spontaneously and naturally, who are playing a lead role in this new social unity—seek a place in which to consult, to manage, and to engage in creative cooperation in every appropriate sector of their lives. As corporate leaders, you must support the vitality that is coming from this new cooperation. Strengthening it and protecting it might well become our principal mission.

Given that perspective, how can we not think of educational institutions as an ideal place for such exchanges?

h) Openness to committed personal and socioreligious experience. Religion is a creative force in human life, in history, and it gives a dynamism to every life that opens itself to experiencing it.

How can it be that in certain educational environments, every subject and every question can be studied except one: God, the excluded; God, the unwelcome?

In the name of a neutrality that everyone knows is impossible, we silence and cut off a dimension of life that, far from being harmful, can contribute greatly to the formation of hearts and to peace in our lives.

We will never learn to respect all persons and to recognize diversity as a road to unity if we suppress legitimate conscientious choices or the open discussion of what flows from another person's view of the world.

It almost seems that the public square is now supposed to be only "lite," frothy, protected from any strongly-held opinions. It seems that the only acceptable approach is one of vagueness and frivolity, or else of approval of the actions of those in power.

Educate, and Then ...? Educate Some More

Looking at the social scene, where no family is free from difficulties—whether internal and external, economic, violence-related or caused by embitterment—we have to ask ourselves: "How is education possible?" But at the same time we cannot but ask, "How can we *not* educate? How can we *not* continue to place our faith in education?"

Education doesn't exist without a teacher, a professor. But neither does it exist without a human pupil. And that becomes relevant when competing structures, curricula, programs, content, evaluations and administrative procedures all battle to be the most important element of education.

Postmodern culture presents youthfulness as the model for the person. You're beautiful only if you look young, and people undergo surgical procedures to erase the marks of time. Beauty is youthful, informal, casual. Our ideal adult is actually an adolescent.

The adolescent is seen as one who has found new ways of feeling, thinking, acting. But at the same time we see him or her lacking in the ability to understand the world in which they live and lacking in any hope for the future. School-based education seems old-fashioned to these young people, meaningless. They think that very little of what the school teaches them is necessary for life in society.

Looking at the past success of their teaching methodology, experienced teachers sometimes find the world of the adolescent distant and hard to understand. They are dealing with adolescents who have no respect for book learning or for teachers who don't understand their questions. The result is a *non-encounter*.

Youth are also tempted to an endless search for pleasure, for the instant and painless satisfaction of their desires, in an ideal world made up only of images. Book learning is seen as not being very attractive—as irrelevant, actually—because it doesn't satisfy the senses or guarantee an improvement in social position, or even a job.

It is not in school that young people find what they're looking for. "Modern" schools are taking in postmodern students, perhaps a little too casually. But that's not all.

Consistency is essential. Trading accusations is a waste of time. As a society we have to cultivate clarity to overcome non-encounter, to avoid wasting energy by building with one hand what we destroy with the other.

Education and Encounter

And what to teach? The diversity and multiplicity of what is knowable is without limit. In this multiplicity, how do we decide what to teach, what to learn? Perhaps there is an answer in the relatively straightforward process of trying to decide on a study plan. Knowing *what* is to be learned doesn't necessarily tell us *why* we learn it or what it is good for, but in the reflective encounters among men and women in the planning process, it is possible that the purpose of education can be accomplished; for the goal of education is formation, that is, the shaping of a life. This process, which naturally respects the intrinsic value of the things to be learned, must also be a path, a path of encounter in which both the teacher and the pupil understand themselves better—better in relation to their present, to their history, to society and to the world.

Education must avoid the risk of becoming simply a distributor of information. It must provide interpretation and evaluation, not just content and methods.

Teacher and student must reach a common understanding that unites them in a search for truth, united not only in what is being studied but also in their integrity and their understanding of existence.

What is necessary is an education that retains what is fundamental as a foundation on which to build.

The True, the Beautiful, the Good exist. The Absolute exists. It can—it *must*— be known and perceived.

We need education that strengthens the fabric of society. Let education be a place of encounter and common commitment in which we learn to be a society, and in which society learns to care for and about its members. We must learn new forms of building the city of mankind.

Not Just Words: Life

All of you—as students, former students, and as parents—know the growing needs of education. Also, as corporate executives, you have truly become associated with the schools by setting up internships and educational projects in the community.

Today I ask you to put into action the concern for education that led you to invite me to this gathering. The welcome you have extended encourages me to ask your support for an initiative of the Parochial Schools Department of the Archdiocese, aimed at giving assistance and support to structurally weak, or weakened, parts of the school system by consolidating the most needy areas through the construction of community centers that will provide services to address diversity, family, poverty, and education.

The Church has been active here, on the shores of the Rio de la Plata, for almost four hundred years. In fact, the first school here was a Jesuit college. And we'd like to say that the Church will always be active in education. The Church wants to be able to offer totally free schooling in the areas of our city where failure rates and other problems are most acute, for example in Lugano, Soldati, la Boca, and Barracas. We are already active in these areas, but we want to increase our presence and support, offering to these children and their families the stability, formation and follow-up that they need

My dear friends, education and the littlest ones in our society expect much from you and us. I know your efforts and the work you are doing. I know as well the enthusiasm and the ability that you can furnish in support of education in our city in this crucial time.

Education and Encounter

A people who wants to exorcize the poverty of emptiness and despair! A people with memory, a memory that is not simply entries in a log! That's what shows the greatness of our people! I see in our Argentinian people a strong sense of their own dignity. It is an awareness created by key events in our history. Our people have a soul; and because we can speak of the soul, we can speak of a vision of life, a way of looking at reality, a conscience. Today, in the midst of conflicts, this people teaches that we mustn't listen to those who want to turn reality into ideas and nothing more. We don't need intellectuals who have no substance or ethicists who have no integrity. Rather, we must call on our wisdom, and on our cultural reserves. We are seeing a real revolution, but one that is internal, and not at all political. A revolution of memory and tenderness, the memory of our founding heroic exploits. And the memory of simple gestures learned in our families. Being faithful to our mission means protecting this ember of memory in our heart, rescuing it from the deceptive ashes of forgetfulness and from the presumptuousness of believing that our country, our city and our family have no history, or that they began only with us. An ember of memory that concentrates, like a log on the fire, the values that make us great: our way of welcoming and defending life, of accepting death, of caring for the poorest of our brethren, of opening our arms to suffering and poverty in a spirit of community, our way of celebrating and praying, our dream of working together and of building up solidarity out of our shared poverty,

We are all invited to help build a culture of encounter, to experience and share in this ferment that, while new, is at the same time a memory that recalls our shining history of sacrifice for one another, our struggle against many slaveries, and our social integration.

We remind ourselves once again that the whole is greater than the sum of its parts, that time is greater than space, that reality is superior to ideas, and that unity is greater than conflict.

In closing, let us ask ourselves a question: "What kind of world will we leave to our children?" Or better, "What kind of children are we giving to our world?"

CHAPTER SEVEN
CHILDREN AT RISK[234]

To the priests, consecrated religious and the lay faithful of the Archdiocese,

My dear brothers and sisters,

The motto of the Thirty-First Youth Pilgrimage to the National Shrine of Luján is: "Mother, help us to care for life." We ask this grace of our mother: Help us to care for all life, all throughout life. We do so in a childlike prayer yet with the confidence that Our Lady gives us. She said to Saint Juan Diego: "Am I not here, I who am your mother?" Knowing that she is here with the tenderness of a mother gives us, her children, the strength to continue to ask her: "Mother, help us to care for life." With this simple prayer in mind, I want to reflect upon how it relates to the life of our city.

In recent years, new realities have appeared on our civic landscape: roadblocks on our streets, demonstrations, homeless people. One of these developments—the most painful in my opinion—involves children. We are hurt and shocked by the wrongful and dangerous victimization of our young boys and girls, our teenagers.

Alone or in groups, there are children and teenagers living on the streets. They beg, they sleep in the subway, in train stations, in building lobbies and arcades, sometimes doing drugs. All these are everyday realities in our cities.

---

[234] Letter, October 1, 2005, Feast of St. Theresa of the Child Jesus, Patron of the Children of the Archdiocese, on the occasion of the Thirty-First Youth Pilgrimage to the National Shrine of Our Lady of Luján, forty-five miles from Buenos Aires.

Children and adolescents searching through trash and garbage late at night looking for cardboard to sell or discarded food that might be their only meal of the day.

Children and youth—often watched by the adults who exploit them by making them do various kinds of licensed or unlicensed jobs—hawking trinkets, cleaning windshields, juggling, opening doors for people exiting their cars, peddling holy cards in the subway.

In Buenos Aires, draft animals are illegal, and if a trash cart is caught being pulled by an animal, cart and horse can be confiscated. But there are hundreds of trash pickers' carts everywhere—I see them every day in the center of town—and since animals can't be used, it is often young boys who push them. Doesn't that make these children draft animals?

The press recently reported on a pedophile ring operating in the neighborhoods of Chacarita, Floresta, Congreso, Recoleta, San Telmo, Montserrat, Nuñez, Palermo and Caballito. Boys and girls between the ages of five and fifteen were being used by adults for sex! Some years back we "rent our garments" when we learned about sex tourism: Europeans going to destinations in Asia for sex, often sex with children. Now we have the same thing here, even in some of our luxury hotels.

Another painful reality is the growing use of children and adolescents in the drug trade. In addition, unscrupulous liquor store owners are complicit in the scandal of increased use of alcohol by underage young people, and even by small children.

Reliable statistics indicate that the majority of our children are poor and that approximately half of the poor are children. These conditions, and projected poverty rates, are such that there will undoubtedly be an increase in malnutrition, environmental degradation, unhealthy living conditions, violence and promiscuity.

All this affects our children's growth, making their personal relationships more difficult and weakening their socialization and integration into the community. As an aside, it is disgusting that some tour companies include in their itineraries for foreigners the shanty towns where poor and needy children live.

Experts in the field have pointed out that entertainment productions, especially what is featured on television, expose our children and youth to an unending stream of programs that debase and trivialize sex, devalue the family, pass off negative values as praiseworthy, celebrate violence, and portray freedom as being directed only toward the satisfaction of one's own desires, without any accountability. These programs, which become paradigms for behavior, are made possible by the passivity of government regulators and the financial backing of complicit sponsors.

This reality speaks to us of an ever more extensive and profound moral degradation that should prompt us to ask how we can recover respect for the life and dignity of our children. We are robbing many of them of their childhood, and we are endangering their future and ours. This is a responsibility that we all share but that weighs more heavily on those who have more power, education and wealth.

If we look at religion, how many children know how to pray? How many have been taught to search out and contemplate the face of their Father in heaven, who loves them with a special love? Not passing on religious values to our children is a great failure that touches a person's very essence.

All these situations shake us, reminding us of our Christian and civic responsibilities, and call us to solidarity as members of a community that we want to be increasingly more human, more worthy, more respectful of human and social dignity.

There is a danger that the more accustomed we become to the circumstances in which our children and youth live, the more those conditions will be viewed with passivity and indifference. Either what is wrongful becomes the norm, or else excessive severity—ostensibly oriented toward the common good—produces repression and increasing control, with legal procedures that go from a reduction in the age of legal responsibility to the removal of children from their families, in effect making poverty itself a crime and promoting arbitrary and abusive incarceration.

We could continue this description, which is really a call for greater awareness. We must become more aware of the desperate conditions our children and young people are living in, and we must respond to their needs in a manner consistent with our personal and social responsibility. We should treat this situation as if we ourselves were being subjected to the laws in question.

We have to recognize that every boy or girl who is marginalized, abandoned or living on the streets, with scant access to education and healthcare, is a living example not only of injustice but also of the breakdown of institutions—the family and its neighborhood network, local charities, the parish, and all the different government agencies. Many of these situations demand an immediate response, but not with a lot of fanfare. The search for, and practical application of, solutions should not be a patchwork exercise. We need a change of heart and mind that leads us to value these children and give them a life worth living, from their mother's womb until they rest in the arms of God their Father, and we must put that approach into practice every day.

We must enter into the heart of God and begin to listen to the voices of the weakest among us—these children and adolescents—and remember the words of the Lord: "Whoever receives one child such as this in My name receives Me."[235] And "See that you do not mistreat one of these little ones, for I say to you that their angels in heaven always look upon the face of My heavenly Father."[236] Their voices, together with the words of the Lord, should inspire us in our commitment and in our actions:

Never should our children be abandoned in our city;

Never should our adolescents and other young people be marginalized in our city;

No Christian, no parish, no governmental agency should be idle or indifferent seeing the crosses that our families and children have to bear;

No selfishness or personal or group interest should reduce the effectiveness of our effort and commitment by weakening the unity and coordination necessary for this urgent and immediate undertaking.

I have written this letter because I am worried and hurt by this situation. I have discussed this matter with several specialists, and with our Diocesan Office for Children, with the Commission for Children and Adolescents at Risk, and with several judges and legislators. I want us never to get used to this new face of our city, to seeing children in such danger. Please open your eyes to this deplorable reality. Today's Herods have different faces, but the situation today is the same as in the Bible: Children are being killed, their smiles are being killed, their hope is being killed ... they are becoming cannon fodder! Let us look with newly-opened eyes at these children in our city and prepare to weep. Look to the Virgin Mary and tell her with weeping hearts: "Mother, help us to watch over life."

---

[235] Mt. 18:5

[236] Mt. 18:10

CHAPTER EIGHT
FAMILY AND COUNTRY[237]

At that time Jesus said in reply, "I give praise to You, Father, Lord of heaven and earth, for although You have hidden these things from the wise and the learned, You have revealed them to the childlike. Yes, Father, such has been Your gracious will. All things have been handed over to Me by My Father. No one knows the Son except the Father, and no one knows the Father except the Son and anyone to whom the Son wishes to reveal Him. Come to Me, all you who labor and are burdened, and I will give you rest. Take My yoke upon you and learn from Me, for I am meek and humble of heart; and you will find rest for yourselves. For My yoke is easy, and My burden light."[238]

This passage of the Gospel surprises us with its intimate prayerfulness. It is almost liturgical. Jesus, who makes Himself small in our eyes, opens Himself to the infinity of God as well as to God's fatherly warmth. Jesus is at rest deep within Himself; He feels Himself both Son and beloved brother among these same little ones who received the Father's love from Him.

That love lifts burdens, sweetens and nurtures, and in it life is no longer a burden. Love creates a community of brothers and sisters that banishes angst and frees our souls from the suffocating weight of our own presumption and stubbornness.

God makes us brothers and sisters in Jesus Christ because His attentive, patient and energizing love frees us from blindness and from the shell of our pride and vanity, allowing us to see how, in that love, a different life is possible.

---

[237] Homily, May 25, 2011, Argentinian National Holiday.
[238] Mt. 11:25-30

Family and Country

Today we want to allow ourselves to be guided by that love to revive the wonderful dream that takes us back to those who've gone before us, those who gave their lives so that we might be here: our brothers and sisters who unified us in our love for our Country with their work and their struggles, who let themselves be inspired by a faith that gave them great generosity and the ability to give of themselves unconditionally.

The Gospel passage speaks to us of humility. To that human smallness that is aware of being small, humility reveals all the potential that is within humanity. Indeed, the more we are aware of our limits and talents, the more we will be free from the blindness of pride. And therefore, as Jesus praises the Father for this revelation to the little ones, we too should praise the Father for having caused the Sun of May[239] to rise on those who believed in the gift of freedom, this freedom that grows in the hearts of a people who risked all for greatness, but never forgot how small they were.

Self-interest and conflicting opinions couldn't kill the seed. It grew in sacrifice, in heroism, and in loving dedication to the building of a nation.

This May holiday reminds us of the boldness of those who became strong despite their humble beginnings. They were not spared sacrifices, hardships, privations, or death during the long journey needed to build a home here for all those of good will who lived in this land.

---

[239] A sun in its splendor is a symbol of Argentina and appears on the Argentinian flag. Its name, the "Sun of May," recalls the 1810 May Revolution that led to Argentina's independence from Spain. (Trans. note)

They did not build this country with arrogant delusions of grandeur, but rather with everyday labor. We build, struggle, fail, and begin again.

A review of these past two hundred years reveals that there have been, as there will always be, petty interests, personal and group agendas, but the only thing that has lasted is what has been built by everybody, for the common good.

Lifting our gaze to the Father as Jesus did, we recognize those people who, today as in the past, contribute and share with humility, and only with humility. They are people who free themselves from the weight of excessive ambition, free to fly, but with solid plans, creativity, and dedication to attain that which is most ennobling.

Remembering them we rediscover ourselves, and we discover how the love of God the Father is always with us in the humble greatness of many individuals.

But we also know that our good Father does not intrude on our liberty; He doesn't interfere or limit our choices. If we choose to dream of self-sufficiency, if we abandon humility by thinking we are something we are not, we will sleep the nightmare of a country that has abandoned its destiny. That will be our fault, and ours alone.

We feel called to ask for the grace to renew our spirits and reawaken our truth. Unlikely as it may seem, our petition is nevertheless full of hope, because he who discovers himself, and "the other," and God, discovers truth, and only the Truth can make us free.[240]

The breath of God that gave us life when He formed us with His hands, we experience again when we feel recognized as His sons

---

[240] Jn 8:33

and daughters. For our spirits, we ask the ability and the willingness to listen, think, and feel in a way that fulfills our vision and longing for greatness—a greatness, however, that is attained with our feet on the ground.

Listen to the word from on high, as Jesus listened. Be hearers so that truth may be revealed while at the same time our pride is laid bare. Listen to the Lord, who inspires great things in the silence of our hearts and in the hearts of our brothers and sisters, our friends, our companions. Rebuild the bonds that join us in a common quest.

This is how the wisdom of our quiet and hard-working people grows and spreads. Their only social identifier is their humbleness.

It is the wisdom of those who carry the Cross of suffering, of injustice—of those who live in the worst conditions yet get up every morning to sacrifice themselves for their families.

It is the wisdom of those who carry the cross of sickness, of suffering, and of loss, willingly, as did Christ.

It is the wisdom of thousands of women and men who wait in lines for the buses that take them to their honest toil, working so they can bring home food for the table, so they can set aside something to make the house a little nicer.

We see our humble greatness in the thousands and thousands of children at school and going back and forth between home and school; we see it in the grandparents, the keepers of folk wisdom, who gather to talk and trade stories.

All these humble ones have to deal with crises and dishonesty. Contempt from the powerful might condemn them to extreme poverty, offer them the suicide of drugs, civil disorder and violence. They might be tempted to the hatred born of vengeful resentment. But they, the humble, whatever be their position and social condition, will call on the wisdom of Him who knows He is the Son of a God who is not distant, of Him who accompanies them with His Cross and who through His Resurrection encourages them to work miracles—those everyday successes that let them enjoy the satisfaction that comes from sharing and celebration.

Those who savor this mystery—the wise who understand smallness—they are the ones who find rest in Him, in the tender embrace of God. Some seek pardon; many others offer up their abilities in various ways in service to the community.

They know that a word full of love, even if it's no more than a gesture, liberates. It liberates us from the yoke that we take on when we try to do the impossible, when we punish ourselves by seeking what is unreachable, when we fall into a depression over unrealized ambitions and recognition, when we endlessly seek affection, or when we grasp at power or wealth. The wisdom of the humble man or woman doesn't need these things. They know they have worth just by being themselves. They feel loved by the Father, their Creator, even in the face of contempt, abandonment, and humiliation.

This is how the Master of Humility taught us, He who willingly carried His Cross to the Passion.

This is why, even after two hundred years of our history, today's holiday asks us once again to reawaken humility in ourselves, the humility to accept what we can do and who we are, and the greatness to share without deception or disguise. Unbridled ambition will do nothing more than make the winner a keeper in acres of wilderness, or king of a desolate wasteland.

The trappings of power and rancorous fights over position trap the soul, covering its sorry emptiness and stifling its ability to offer creative solutions that inspire confidence. They lead to compulsive pride in its most unattractive manifestation—unreliability.

The unreliable person, full of him or herself, is someone who doesn't know the difference between scheming and organizing, between skirmishes and campaigns, between personal advantage and a vision of greatness. Since they can't stand themselves, they need to intimidate others, and they drag out discussions of perfectly clear matters by disputing accepted facts. With nothing of substance to add, they simply try to give orders. They live by raising doubts, making everything relative, stepping out of line, and they survive by remaining adolescent forever.

None of us is free from inconstancy. Perhaps it is an Argentinian weakness. But its punishment comes in the form of an inability to love and be loved, to listen to the other, to accept responsibility, to suffer with others, to have a spirit of community, to accompany others, to recognize limits and differences, and to accept one's own limitations and role.

People who are unreliable are also lonely—even if they have someone to keep them company, even if they can make others show them respect and be subservient, even if they seek to seduce or impress others with their behavior or their words.

Is it because of our own petty and erratic insecurity that we build walls, whether of wealth, power, or unpunished violence? If so, the humility of Jesus lightens our burdens and lifts the yoke of vanity and insecurity. He invites us to have confidence, to share in order to include.

My dear brothers and sisters, Jesus invites us to lift the burden that is ourselves, the burden of those pretenses, false beliefs and superficial solutions that all of us like to try. He invites us instead to rebuild our confidence in the benefits of shared, long-term fraternal cooperation.

145

In this we follow the example of our humble fellow-countrymen. They were heroes, known and unknown, who felt themselves to be children of God and of our homeland.

As He Himself suggests, we have to be trusting as children, just as He was—He who spared neither strength not commitment even when He saw no results.

Fraternity in love, living as Jesus did, lifts us up and renders our yoke light. Certainly, no one these days is without fault; no one gets involved in shady deals without getting dirty, but Jesus invites us to abandon the pigpens of corruption. God always pardons us and lifts us up. God never tires of forgiving—it is we who tire of asking pardon.

Disintegration is the result of an arrogant "everyone for himself" attitude, of taking advantage of disorder to grab at power when the opportunity presents itself.

From the disinterestedness that is born of knowing we are little but confident, we reap the joy of building together the greatness of our country.

And together, let us offer a prayer from our hearts: Jesus Christ, Lord of history, give us the grace to know how to rejoice in the brotherhood and humble friendship that inspire us to build together. We too are children of Your Father and our Father. Our hearts are hardened by rivalries and pettiness; soften them before it's too late. Let us not listen, prideful and ambitious, to the fears that empty us and make us hollow, rather let us take on the easy yoke of sharing without the need to control. It is our duty in justice to our brothers and sisters, to ourselves, and to You.

Mary of Luján, who remained in our land as our mother, a gift who gives us God's tenderness with your presence, your hands, your silence: Hear the cry of your people for "justice long awaited." Listen to the silent lament of those who destroy themselves because they have lost all hope, who are day workers paid only with leftovers, who can't remember the "joy of being alive."

Your face tells us that there is no misfortune that can stop us, because looking on your Son, Jesus, the way you do, we find peace even in our most difficult moments.

From Him we want to recover the humility that He taught us and that restores our confidence.

CHAPTER NINE

SOCIAL DEBT[241]

In this presentation I will try to give an overview of the doctrine of the Church about "social debt."

In November 2008 the bishops of Argentina declared "social debt" to be Argentina's greatest financial liability. It affects all of us, and its payment cannot be delayed.[242] We must therefore become keenly aware of this debt that we owe to the society in which we live. A part of that task will be to deepen our understanding of the Social Teaching of the Church about social debt.

We're not dealing simply with an economic or statistical problem. Social debt is primarily a moral problem that touches our most basic dignity.[243]

As our bishops have said, "Social debt is the sum of the shortfalls that create a significant risk for adequate sustenance, personal dignity and opportunities for human development."[244]

Social debt is also an existential debt, a calling into question the very meaning of life. Restoring an understanding of the meaning of life will require the individual to have a sense of "belonging to" what he or she does, and to the social groups where activities are

---

[241] Inaugural Conference at the Seminar on "Social Debt" organized by EPOCA, September 30, 2009.

[242] *Towards a Bicentennial in Justice and Solidarity* (2010-2016), 5. Document issued by the Argentinian bishops at the conclusion of the Ninety-sixth Plenary Assembly of the Bishops' Conference of Argentina, Pilar, November 14, 2008. Referred to herein as the "Pilar Document" and cited as "PrD."

[243] *Ibid.*

[244] *Deepening Social Pastoral Ministry*, Letter of the Episcopate as part of the 88th Plenary Meeting, San Miguel, November 11, 2004.

carried out. That is why, as Durkheim[245] says, all existential emptiness is traceable to an individual's becoming separated from his or her social environment; in other words, to a lack of that sense of belonging that is essential to identity. "Having an identity" basically implies "belonging."

Consequently, to be able to pay down our social debt we will have to reweave our social fabric and repair our social connections.

A study produced by the Catholic University of Argentina defines "social debt" as all those privations and deficiencies that are related to personal and social human needs; in other words, as a violation of the right to develop a full, active and worthy life in a context of freedom, equal opportunity and social progress.

The ethical foundation that allows us to judge social debt as immoral, unjust and unlawful rests on a societal acknowledgment of the grave harm its consequences do to life, to the value of life and, therefore, to human dignity.

According to the bishops of Argentina, social debt's "greatest immorality lies in the fact that it exists in a country that has the ability to avoid or correct such harm but, unfortunately, appears to have chosen to exacerbate inequality even further."[246]

---

[245] French sociologist Émile Durkheim (1858-1917), who, in his book *Le Suicide* (1897) wrote: "[When the individual] is individualized beyond a certain point, if he is separated too radically from other beings, people or things, he ends up torn away from the very sources that would normally provide nourishment, and he has nothing left to hold on to. By creating a vacuum around himself he can do nothing but reflect on his own misery. The only object of his meditation is the nothingness that it contains and the sorrow that follows it. A life without direction is a life without social roots." *El Suicidio*, Shapire Editor, Buenos Aires, 1971, p. 225.

[246] *Deepening Social Pastoral Ministry,* Letter of the Episcopate as part of the 88th Plenary Meeting, San Miguel, November 11, 2004.

This debt is owed by all those who have the moral or political responsibility for safeguarding and promoting the dignity of persons and their rights, and it is owed to those members of society whose rights are violated.

"Human rights," as the *Santo Domingo Document* says, "are violated not only by terrorism, repression, and murder, but also by the existence of extreme poverty and unjust economic structures that create great inequalities."[247]

Social Debt as an Anthropological Question

The fundamental principle in the Social Teaching of the Church that underlies a recognition of social debt is the inviolable dignity of the person and his or her rights. It is a dignity that each of us possesses and that we recognize in the poor and in those who are excluded.[248]

From this recognition comes the principle that directs human activity: Individual human beings are the foundation, the cause and the end of every social institution;[249] as Blessed Paul VI and St. John Paul II say, *every person, the whole person, and all persons.*

For this reason, we cannot fairly answer the challenge of eliminating exclusion and poverty if the poor remain objects— recipients of government or private paternalistic welfare initiatives—rather than doers for whom government and society create conditions that promote and safeguard their rights and enable them to create their own futures.

---

[247] SDD 167

[248] Pontifical Council for Justice and Peace, *Compendium of the Social Doctrine of the Church*, 153. Cited in this Volume as "CSDC."

[249] St. John XXIII: *Mater et Magistra*, Encyclical Letter on recent developments of the social question in the light of Christian doctrine, May 14, 1961, 219.

In the Encyclical *Centesimus Annus*, St. John Paul II pointed out the need to "abandon a mentality in which the poor—as individuals and as peoples—are considered a burden, as irksome intruders trying to consume what others have produced. The poor ask for the right to share in enjoying material goods and to use their capacity for work, thus creating a world that is more just and prosperous for all." [250]

Following this line of thought, one has to say that the "social question"—social debt—has been transformed into an anthropological question. [251]

Why? As St. John Paul II explains: "Even prior to the logic of a fair exchange of goods and the forms of justice appropriate to it, there exists something which is due to the person because he is a person, by reason of his lofty dignity. That 'something' necessarily includes the possibility of survival and of making an active contribution to the common good of humanity." [252]

In this sense, "It is a strict duty of justice and truth not to allow fundamental human needs to remain unsatisfied, and not to allow those burdened by such needs to perish. It is also necessary to help needy persons to acquire skills, to enter the workplace, and to develop their skills in order to make the best use of their capacities and resources." [253]

Causes of the Growth of Poverty and Exclusion

---

[250] St. John Paul II, *Centesimus Annus*, Encyclical Letter on the centenary of *Rerum Novarum*, May 1, 1991, 28. Cited in this volume as "CA."

[251] Benedict XVI, *Caritas in Veritate*, Encyclical Letter on integral human development in charity and truth, June 29, 2009, 75. Cited in this volume as "CV."

[252] CA 34

[253] *Ibid.*

Social exclusion does radical harm to one's sense of belonging in society. The excluded are no longer faced with the question of being "behind" or at the margins, or powerless. They are "out." The excluded—to whom we are social debtors—are not only "exploited," they are "excess" and "disposable."[254]

During an Apostolic Visit to Germany, St. John Paul II said, that current culture tends to offer lifestyles that are not natural and that offend human dignity.[255] Contemporary culture—heedless of the value of the human person—has looked to the idols of power, wealth, and fleeting pleasure for its standards of behavior and its criteria for social organization.

The economic and social crisis and the consequent growth of poverty are caused by policies inspired by variations of economic theory that—to the detriment of the dignity of the individual and of peoples—consider profit and market forces to be absolutes. In this context, we repeat our conviction that the loss of the sense of justice and the lack of respect for others have become more pronounced and have led to inequality.[256]

The consequence of this situation is the concentration of natural, financial and informational wealth in the hands of a few, with resulting increases in inequality and exclusion.[257]

As we analyze the situation further, we see that even though economic hardship is the result of many factors, poverty today is not a chance phenomenon. It is rather the result of economic, social and political conditions and structures.[258]

---

[254] AD 65

[255] Mainz, November 16, 1980.

[256] *Naviga Mar Adentro* 34, Concluding Document of the 85th Plenary Assembly of the Argentinian Bishops' Conference, San Miguel, May 31, 2003.

[257] AD 22

[258] PD 29

As St. John Paul II told us, poverty in our countries is often caused by processes that, because they are materialistic rather than authentically humanistic, result, at the international level, in the rich getting richer while "next door" the poor are getting poorer.[259]

This is a situation that demands personal conversion and thoroughgoing structural change that is consistent with the legitimate desires of the people for true social justice.[260]

Social Debt and Social Justice

The Second Vatican Council said that "excessive economic and social differences between the members of the one human family or population groups cause scandal and militate against social justice, equity, the dignity of the human person, and social and international peace."[261]

Starting in the first half of the twentieth century, the idea of social justice has become part of the Church's Social Teaching. The Church teaches that social justice is an authentic development of general justice, being closely connected to what is called the "social question."[262] It addresses the social, political, economic and, above

---

[259] St. John Paul II, Inaugural Address at the Palafox Major Seminary, Puebla, Mexico, January 28, 1979. Herein referred to as the "Palafox Document" and cited as "PxD."

[260] PD 29

[261] GS 29

[262] Beginning in the nineteenth century, discussion and debate with respect to significant changes in society as a result of industrialization and urbanization took place under the heading "Social Question." See, for example, the following link:

http://iroesner.files.wordpress.com/2013/02/industrial-revolution.pdf (Trans. note)

all, structural aspects of problems and of their solutions.[263] Benedict XVI, in his Encyclical *Deus Caritas Est*, says, "Justice is both the aim and the intrinsic criterion of all politics."[264]

Social justice forbids one class to exclude another in the sharing of benefits. In the words of Pope Pius XI, "The riches that economic-social developments constantly increase ought to be so distributed among individual persons and classes that the common advantage of all, which Leo XIII had praised, will be safeguarded; in other words, that the common good of all society will be kept inviolate."[265]

Social justice looks to the common good, which at present consists principally of the defense of human rights. As presented in paragraphs 388-398 of CSDC, these "constitute an objective norm on which positive law is based and which cannot be ignored by the political community, because in both its existential being and its final purpose the human person precedes the political community."[266]   And—in the context of social debt—a consideration of the common good necessarily includes a consideration of community: "The Christian vision of political society places paramount importance on the value of community, both as a model for organizing life in society and as a style of everyday living."[267]

Political-economic Activity, Integral Development, and Social Debt

---

[263] CSDC 201

[264] DCE 28

[265] Pius XI, *Quadragesimo Anno* 57, Encyclical Letter on the restoration of social order in perfect conformity with the Gospel law on the fortieth anniversary of the Encyclical *Rerum Novarum* of Leo XIII, March 15, 1931.

[266] CSDC 392

[267] *Ibid.*

A consideration of poverty requires us to become aware of its "social and economic dimension"[268] because it is primarily a human problem. It has a first name and a last name. It has feelings and faces. Not caring that there are people who are excluded or considered intrinsically less than others is a serious moral failing that diminishes human dignity and undermines social harmony and peace.[269]

There is an inverse relationship between human development and social debt. We're not dealing simply with economic development, but rather with a total development that involves the growth of all the capabilities of the individual. Less development means more social debt. Thus, development and inequality must be dealt with together, not separately; and if people become inured to inequality, or if they consider it just one more political football, the fight for equal opportunity will leave the political discussion behind and become simply a struggle to survive.

"Economic activity cannot solve all social problems through the simple application of business logic. It needs to be directed towards the pursuit of the common good, for which the political community must take responsibility. Therefore, it must be kept in mind that grave imbalances are produced when economic action, conceived merely as an engine for wealth creation, is detached from political action, conceived as a means for pursuing justice through redistribution."[270]

"The Church's social doctrine holds that authentically human social relationships of friendship, solidarity and reciprocity can also be conducted within economic activity, and not only outside it

---

[268] PrD 5

[269] *Dealing Appropriately with the Current Situation,* 6b. The Bishops of Argentina, San Miguel, November 11, 2000.

[270] CV 36

or 'after' it. The economic sphere is neither ethically neutral, nor inherently inhuman and opposed to society. It is part and parcel of human activity, and precisely because it is human, it must be structured and governed in an ethical manner."[271]

Blessed Paul VI, referring to the use of capital, called for serious reflection on the harm that can be caused to one's own country by transfers of capital to other countries solely for a greater return on investment.[272] St. John Paul II was of the view that, subject to prevailing unavoidable economic and political conditions, a decision to invest abroad—that is, to offer people an opportunity to reap value from their own labor—can include among its motivations a desire to help and a trust in Providence, which would demonstrate the human qualities of the investor.

Caritas in Veritate emphasized that such an approach is *"still valid today, despite the fact that the capital markets have been significantly deregulated, and that modern technological thinking might consider investment to be a merely technical act, not a human and ethical one. There is no reason to deny that a certain amount of capital can do good if invested abroad rather than at home. Yet the requirements of justice must be safeguarded, with due consideration for the way in which the capital was generated and the harm to individuals that will result if it is not used where it was produced.*

"What should be avoided is a speculative use of financial resources that yields to the temptation of seeking only short-term profit, without regard for the long-term sustainability of the enterprise, its benefit to the real economy, and attention to the advancement (in suitable and appropriate ways) of further

---

[271] *Ibid.*

[272] PP 24. Blessed Paul VI, Encyclical Letter *Populorum Progressio* on the need to promote the development of peoples, March 26, 1967.

economic initiatives in countries that are in need of development. It is true that the export of investments and skills can benefit the populations of the receiving country. ...

"Yet it is not right to export these things—merely for the sake of obtaining advantageous conditions or, worse, for purposes of exploitation—without making a real contribution to local society by helping to bring about a robust productive and social system, an essential factor for stable development."[273]

Capital also has a native country, one might say.

"In this regard, the need for government that is active, transparent, effective and efficient, and that promotes the public welfare, is a new choice for our poorest and most excluded brothers.

"Confirming and enhancing the choice of that preferential love for the poor[274] *that comes from our faith in Jesus Christ,*[275] *will require us to take care of urgent needs and at the same time work with other agencies and institutions to put in place structures that are more just. Also required are new structures that promote credible coexistence."*[276]

Conclusion

"Social debt" needs social justice. Together, let us call to this task stakeholders: particularly governments, political leaders, the world of banking and finance, entrepreneurs, the food and agriculture industry, corporate leaders, unions, the media, as well as churches and other members of civil society.

---

[273] CV 40b
[274] AD 396
[275] PxD 3; AD 393-394
[276] PrD 18b

Consider that, according to various sources, Argentinians hold abroad approximately one hundred and fifty billion dollars, in addition to funds that are in the country but that are outside the banking system. In addition, the media report that another two billion dollars leaves the country each month.

I wonder, and I ask you: What can we do to put these resources at the service of our country, to pay off our social debt and create the conditions for comprehensive development for all?

Social debt is owed to millions of Argentinians, mostly children and young people who need our ethical, cultural and supportive response. This forces us to work to change the structural causes and the personal or corporate attitudes that have created this situation. Through dialogue, we need to reach agreements that will allow us to transform the painful reality that we are referring to when we speak of social debt.

When the Church recognizes and talks about social debt, it shows once again its love and preferential option for the poor and marginalized,[277] with whom Jesus especially identified.[278] It does so in the light of the primacy of charity, attested to by Christian tradition, begun by the Pilgrim Church,[279] and following prophetic tradition.[280]

It is essential for the Church to address the problem of social debt because men and women, especially the poor, are the way of the Church—the way of Jesus Christ.

---

[277] Benedict XVI, *Fighting Poverty to Build Peace.* Message for the World Day of Peace, January 1, 2009.

[278] Mt. 25:40

[279] Acts 4:32; 1 Cor 16:1; 2 Cor 8:9; Ga. 2:10

[280] Is 1:11-17; Jer. 7: 4-7; Am. 5:21-25

CHAPTER TEN

MARY, THE WOMAN
WHO WELCOMED AND ACCOMPANIES LIFE[281]

Someone once told me that the Solemnity of the Annunciation is the most glorious day of the year because that's the day when God began His earthly journey with us. God is welcomed by Mary; Mary's womb became a sanctuary protected by the Holy Spirit, protected by the shadow of God. From the moment of the Annunciation, Mary strikes out on a path, a path of accompanying the life that she had just conceived, the life of Jesus. She waits for Him with great dreams, like every expectant mother, but difficulties arise even before He's born. Yet, she continues to accompany His life in spite of its troubles. Almost ready to give birth, she has to face a journey to Bethlehem in obedience to a law, a Roman law, and she obeys. She respects the law. The baby is born, but not where you might expect—practically on the street, in a stable, no room for Him anywhere else, laid in a manger. But Mary accepts and accompanies all of this.

After the immense joy she feels in welcoming the shepherds and the wise men, with their universal recognition of Jesus, come threats of death and of exile. And Mary accompanies their exile. Afterwards, she accompanies His return, His education and His growth. She accompanies a life that grows, with its difficulties, its persecution. She accompanies His Passion, and His loneliness as He is tortured all through the night. She stands at the foot of the Cross and accompanies the death of her Son. In her profound solitude, she does not lose hope and, full of joy, she accompanies His Resurrection. But her work does not end there, because Jesus

---

[281] Homily at a Mass for Life, March 25, 2011.

entrusts the infant Church to her, and from that moment she has accompanied the Church, and life.

Mary, the woman who welcomed life and accompanied it to the end, with all the problems that arose and all the joys that life gave her. Mary, the woman who on a day like today welcomed life and accompanied it to its fullness. She hasn't finished yet because she continues by accompanying us in the life of the Church to keep us moving forward. The woman of silence, of patience, who bears sorrow, who faces up to difficulties, and who knows how to rejoice greatly in the joys of her Son.

Pope Benedict XVI proclaimed 2011 as the Year of Life, and today when we remember the beginning of Christ's life on Earth, the Year of Life begins and takes its deepest meaning from the life that Mary carried and accompanied. In this Year of Life, I believe it will do us good to ask ourselves how we welcome life, how we accompany life, because sometimes we are not aware how fragile life is. Perhaps we don't appreciate the dangers that threaten the life of a person from conception until death. Today, looking at Mary, who accompanies life, the question I would like to ask you is this: Do we know how to accompany life? The life of our young people, of children who are our own, and of children who are not? Do we know how to encourage our youth? Do we know where to put limits on their education? And the young people who are not ours—who are, to put it delicately, "misbegotten" and roaming the streets—do they concern us as well? They are life! The breath of God is in them! Or am I more concerned about my pets, who since they have no free will are simply following their instincts in giving me what I interpret as affection? Do I ever think that what I spend on pet care could mean food and education for a child who has neither? Do I nurture the life of children as they grow? Am I concerned about who their friends are? Do I want them to grow up adult and free? Do I know how to educate my children for freedom? Do I worry about what they are doing in their free time? Sometimes, when we learn about what they do on their high school graduation trips, we wonder whether we are accompanying life or whether we're simply letting them run wild for a few weeks. Do I pay attention to all of this? And life continues to grow ... and Mary continues to accompany life ... Do I accompany it as she does? And your parents? Your grandparents? Your in-laws? Do you accompany them? Do you worry about them? Do you visit them? Sometimes, painful as it is, they need to live in a senior-care facility because of health or family problems; but, once they are there, do you give up a Saturday or Sunday to be with them? Do you take care of life that is flickering out but that gave life to you?

In this Year of Life, the Pope wants us to look at the whole course of life. Mary is there each step of the way, just as she took care of a life from its beginning and continues to look after it in us, the pilgrim Church. The worst condition we can be in is to lack the love to take care of life, and Mary gives us a model of total love. If there is no love, there is no room for life. Without love, there is egotism, and we twist all around trying to pat ourselves on the back. Today we ask Mary to give us the love that will enable us to take care of life. The love ... and the courage! Some may say: "But Father, in this global civilization that even seems apocalyptic, how can we bring love to the many conflicting situations we face and take care of life from its beginning to its end?" The great Pope Pius XI gave a very stern answer: "The worst things that can happen to us are not the negative aspects of a civilization; the worst that can happen is for good people to have trouble staying awake."

Do you have the courage to take the path that Mary took, to take care of life from its beginning to its end? Or are you having trouble staying awake? And if so, what is putting you to sleep? Mary did not let her love grow sleepy! So today we ask her: "Mother, make us truly love. Don't let us grow sleepy or seek refuge in the thousand and one sedative-hypnotics our decadent civilization tempts us with."

Amen.

CHAPTER ELEVEN
EUTHANASIA AND ABORTION[282]

Euthanasia

Bergoglio:

Our [Catholic] morality also says that one must do the necessary, the ordinary, in cases where the end is near. One must provide for the quality of life. The value of medicine, in terminal cases, does not consist in making someone live three days or three months longer, but rather in enabling the person to suffer as little as possible. There is no obligation to use extraordinary means to prolong life. Doing so might go against the dignity of the person. Active euthanasia is something else; it is killing. I think that these days covert euthanasia is common: Government or private providers will pay up to a certain amount for treatment, but then they say, "The Lord will provide." The elderly are not taken care of properly, they are disposable. Sometimes medicine and ordinary care is withheld, and that's what kills the patient.

Abortion

Bergoglio:

The moral problem of abortion is of a pre-religious nature because the genetic code of a human being is present at the moment of conception. A human being is already there. I separate the question of abortion from any religious idea. It is a scientific question. To not allow the continued development of a being that

---

[282] Excerpted from *Sobre el Cielo y la Tierra*, co-authored by Cardinal Bergoglio and Rabbi Dr. Abraham Skorka, Libro Editorial Sudamericana, 2010. Rabbi Skorka (b. 1950) is Rector of the Seminario Rabínico Latinoamericano Marshall T. Meyer, and is the Rabbi of the Masorti Olami Community Benei Tikva, in Buenos Aires. (Trans. note)

already has a complete human genetic code is not ethical. The right to life is the first of all human rights. Abortion is killing someone who can't defend him or herself.

CHAPTER TWELVE
DIVORCE AND SAME-SEX MARRIAGE[283]

Divorce
Bergoglio:

The question of divorce is different from the question of same-sex marriage. The Church has always rejected divorce, but it is true that there are distinct anthropological antecedents to the question. In the 1980's, the debate had a more religious character because matrimony until death separates the spouses is a very strong value in Catholicism. Today, however, Catholic teaching reminds the faithful who are divorced and remarried that even though they are living in a situation at the margin of what marriage indissolubility and the Sacrament of Matrimony demand, they are not excommunicated and they are asked to integrate themselves into the life of their parish. The Orthodox churches have an even greater openness with respect to divorce. In that 1980's debate, there was opposition to divorce, but is was more nuanced. There were extreme positions that not everyone shared. Some said it was better not to allow divorce, while others, from a policy point of view, were more favorable to dialogue.

Same-Sex Marriage
Bergoglio:

To define it, I would use the expression *anthropological regression* because it would weaken an institution that is thousands of years old and that reflects nature and anthropology. Fifty years ago "living together" was not as common as it is now, and the expression was clearly pejorative. Later, the situation

---

283 See footnote 282 above.

165

changed; and today, although from the religious point of view it is not right, living together before marriage does not have the social stigma it had fifty years ago. It is a sociological fact, but one that certainly lacks the fullness and greatness of matrimony, which has been a value from time immemorial and deserves to be defended. For this reason, we warn against its possible devaluation; and before a law is changed, serious reflection on what is at stake is called for. What you [Rabbi Skorka] have just pointed out—the Bible's natural law basis for matrimony as the union of man and woman—is important for us [Christians] as well. There have always been homosexuals. The island of Lesbos was known as a place where homosexual women lived. But never in history has it happened that [same-sex unions] were sought to be given the same status as matrimony. We know that in times of great change, the phenomenon of homosexuality increased. But our present times are the first in which the legal question of making same-sex unions the equivalent of matrimony has been raised. I consider this a negative value and an anthropological regression. I say this because it transcends the religious issue; it is anthropological. If there is a private union, no third party, nor society as a whole, is affected. But, if a same-sex couple are considered married and can adopt children, the children could be affected. Everyone needs a male father and a female mother who help shape his or her identity. ...

Bergoglio:

I insist that our [Catholic] opinion about marriage between persons of the same sex is not based on religion but rather on anthropology. When the Head of Government of the City of Buenos

Aires, Mauricio Macri, did not appeal the decision of a trial judge who authorized a [same-sex] wedding, I felt I had to say something, to give an orientation. I felt obligated to express my opinion. It was the first time in my eighteen years as a bishop that I objected to a government official's decision. If you analyze the two statements I made, you will see that at no time did I mention homosexuals or make any disparaging reference to them. The first statement said that the judge's decision was troubling because it evidenced a clear disregard for the law. A trial judge cannot change the Civil Code, and he was changing it. In addition, I pointed out the fact that Macri, who as Head of Government is the guardian of the laws, had forbidden any appeal of the decision. Macri told me that he was acting on his convictions. I know, I respect his convictions, but a Head of Government has no right to give his personal convictions the force of law. At no time did I speak pejoratively about homosexuals, but I did intervene on a point of law. ...

It's often argued that it would be better for a child to be raised by a same-sex couple than in an orphanage or an institution. Neither solution is optimal. The problem is that the government isn't doing what it should. One has to look at the cases of children who are confined to certain institutions where rehabilitation is the least frequent outcome. There need to be civil society institutions, churches and other types of entities that take responsibility for these children. The adoption process, which takes forever, must also be made more efficient so that these children can have a home. But let's not try to correct one governmental mistake with another. The question must be studied in depth. Rather than passing a marriage law that enables same-sex couples to adopt, it would be better to improve existing adoption law, which is excessively bureaucratic and, as now administered, facilitates corruption....

Part of the great adventure [of matrimony], as you [Rabbi Skorka] say, is figuring each other out. There was a priest who used to say that God made us man and woman to need each other—and to *knead* each other. When preaching at weddings, I like to say to the groom that he has to make his bride a real woman, and to the bride that she has to make her husband a real man.

CHAPTER THIRTEEN

MARY: CLOSE TO THE CROSSES OF THOSE WHOSE LIFE IS PAIN[284]

We heard just now that the Mother of Jesus stood at the foot of His Cross.

She was there, caring for life. She stood at the Cross, and she continues to stand near the crosses of those who have pain in their lives. Wherever there is a cross in the heart of one of her children, our mother is there. The Gospel describes this scene in few words but reveals the deep love between Mother and Son. The Blessed Mother looks at her Son, and her Son looks back and gives her to all of us as our mother. Jesus hands over His life and seeks in His mother the one who will take care of many lives, of our lives so in need of protection. In that moment when Jesus speaks to His mother in His utter loneliness, completely abandoned, all He has is her affection and her understanding look. And He entrusts to her the task of giving that affection and that mother's understanding look to every one of us in our most difficult moments. She was there as a mother and she stood by her Son. She knew Him from the moment she welcomed Him into her womb. She felt Him from that moment and believed in Him from the time of the Angel's proclamation. She waited for that Life just as the entire people of believers waited. And that is why she kept all these things in her heart.

As Mary teaches, we must always take care of life. And we must take care of it with the same tenderness that she showed— from His first moment in her womb till His last breath. Taking care of life means sowing hope! A people that takes care of life is a

---

284 Homily at the Youth Pilgrimage to the Shrine of Luján, October 2, 2011.

people that sows hope. Take care of the life of children and the elderly, the beginning and end of life. A people that does not take care of its children and its elderly has begun to be a people in decline. Take care of children and the elderly because in them is contained the future of a people: children because they are the strength that will carry a country forward, the elderly because they are the treasure of wisdom that is poured out on that strength. Strength and wisdom. Taking care of life means sowing hope. Mary took care of Jesus from His infancy, and she takes care of us who are her children, even from our own infancy.

In the Gospel, we see Jesus' concern for life when He says, "Let us take care of all of these people,"[285] and that is what we are experiencing now in this holy place. Here we receive care from our mother. She waits for us. And today, since the Church is undergoing restoration, she has come outside to wait for us, and she wants to be with us.

This is the place where our people have chosen to consecrate their lives, to bring their children as Mary and Joseph did when they brought their Child to the Temple. Mothers and fathers come here in family pilgrimage to present their children, to consecrate them and have them baptized, because they want the Blessed Mother to be present and take care of their children. And this is the reason for our pilgrimage, which brings to her the prayers and intentions of the youngest and the oldest, those whom our Blessed Mother has received and protected throughout the centuries. She knelt by the manger and stood by the Cross; she protects and accompanies every life and in particular the lives that are the most defenseless. And she does so today, when we ask her to teach us

---

[285] See Mt. 14:15-21; Mt. 15:32-39; Mk. 6:35-44; Mk. 8:1-9; Lk. 9:12-17; Jn. 6:1-13.

how to protect life, how to watch over the lives of those who are the least protected, who are the most defenseless.

Dear Mary of Luján, your children feel that you care for them. You know them all, dear Mother, these children who have come on foot to your house. Some weren't able to come but are here in spirit. This occasion and its meaning make us all realize we are a people whom you protect. Dear Mother, we ask the same for all those who couldn't come, for those who have come in pilgrimage beginning yesterday morning, and for those who will continue to come as pilgrims until tomorrow morning. Let no one feel alone or abandoned, dear Mother; let them all find a place in your house. This is the reason, Mother, that you are here, to take care of the lives of your people. You are here to take care of the lives of your people! We ask you to teach us how to stay the course, to continue your care and, as your children, to imitate you in taking care of life. We ask you to teach us how to be silent and, like you, to look upon your children, who are our brothers and sisters. And, here in your house, we reconsecrate ourselves so that your love never fails us, the love that takes care of life.

Mother, help us to take care of life. We've come all this way to your house because we need to ask this of you. You are present here and welcome us in front of your sanctuary. With the joy of this encounter we reconsecrate ourselves and ask you to watch over your children, to take care of your pilgrim people so that it always enjoys your protection. Mother, do not forget us. Take us by the hand and never leave us. And all together, three times, we ask you:

Mother, help us to take care of life.
Mother, help us to take care of life.
Mother, help us to take care of life.

CHAPTER FOURTEEN
CAIN, WHERE IS YOUR BROTHER?
HUMAN TRAFFICKING AND SLAVERY[286]

Today, in this city, we need to hear God calling out: "Cain, where is your brother?" Let that question be heard in every neighborhood in our city, let it penetrate our hearts and especially the hearts of today's Cains. Some of you might ask, "What brother?" I'll tell you. The one who is a slave! The one you are killing every day in hidden sweatshops, in prostitution rings, in the shacks where you hide the children you send out as beggars that you use as lookouts in your drug deals, that you force to steal or to sell their bodies. Who is your brother? The one who has to work, off the books, picking trash because he has no papers? Where is your brother? When we hear this question, do we do what the priest in the Gospel parable did when he pretended not to see the robbery victim lying beaten by the side of the road? Do we do what the Levite did, looking the other way as he passed the same man? "Not my problem, it's someone else's job." No!—it's everybody's problem, because in this city there is a structure of human trafficking that is both "organized and degenerate" (as one government official recently described it)— degenerate and organized crime!

Who is your brother? You who act like just another onlooker, pretending to be thinking about something else, saying, "Not my problem!" and making no room in your heart. Who is your brother? The slave! Your brother is anyone in this city who suffers the evils I just named, because *this city is a wide-open city*, open to

---

[286] Homily at the Fifth Mass for the Victims of Human Trafficking, September 25, 2012.

everybody, open to people looking for slaves, looking for plunder. Just as in a city that is declared "*open*" and subject to pillage when it surrenders in war, these criminals are plundering the lives of our young people! The lives of our workers! The lives of our families! These traffickers—! No, let's not curse them, let's pray instead that they hear God asking: *Where is your brother?*

And you, trafficker, we ask you: Why are you doing this? You'll get nothing out of this but hands dripping with blood from the evil you've done. And speaking of blood, that's how you'll end up— taking a bullet from one of your rivals. That's how the gangs do it! Trafficker, where is your brother? Your brother! Your flesh and blood! Don't you realize that if you make someone a slave, you make yourself a slave as well—and that the Son of God became flesh and blood for both of you?

The greatest grace we can receive today is to weep in our hearts. Lord, here's what we want: Change the hearts of these slave-traders. Change them! Change these people who come to our *open city* to see what they can plunder, whose life they can snuff out, what family they can destroy, what children they can sell, what girls they can ruin. We're not here today to protest; we're here to pray, in the open, in the public square, in an *open city* where anyone at all can come to find a slave.

All of us are here to pray to Jesus for the grace to not get distracted. "But Father, what can I do about the gangs?" Pray! Knock on the Tabernacle door! If you know something, say something. Don't look the other way. It could be your own son or your own daughter who ends up a slave overnight, or it could be you yourself. A while back, I had the joy of baptizing two girls who were the children of a couple who had been freed from a slave sweatshop. Lord, you gave us this favor; give us others so that we can free more, so that we can bring home all those who are being held captive and exploited in slavery.

Lord, grant that we may see converted to You the hearts of the men and women who exploit and enslave their brothers and sisters. That's what we ask today for this *open city* where so many are enslaved. To us who know the truth, grant the grace not to add ourselves to the ranks of the distracted; and to those who enslave, oppress, and suffocate the joy of so many people, grant change of heart.

Amen.

CHAPTER FIFTEEN

HAND IN HAND WITH MARY
STAY CLOSE TO LIFE[287]

The Prodigal Son and the Merciful Father
Luke 15:1-3, 11-32.

The theme for today is "Hand in Hand with Mary, Stay Close to Life." Accompany life so that it grows, surround life to protect it, welcome life as Jesus did. We can't pick and choose among the lives that draw close to ours; we can't act like the Pharisees who murmured against Jesus, saying, "He welcomes sinners and eats with them." Jesus welcomed life as He found it, not just life in fancy clothes.

Jesus said, "This is life and I accept it." It's like soccer: To block a penalty kick, you have to lunge where it's kicked. You can't choose the direction it's going to be kicked in. That's life, and you have to accept it, even if you don't like it.

The father in the Gospel story had given life to his son, watched him grow, and worked to earn great wealth that the son would inherit. But faced one day with his son's childish whim and foolish decision, he let his son go out on his own. He had given him advice, it wasn't listened to. He sold his property to give money to his son. He knew his son would waste it, but that was the situation that life presented this father. Certainly he would have had a talk with the son and given him advice, but in the end he let the son choose. And the son left.

Then, in the Gospel story, the father at last saw the son coming home. He saw from a distance because he would go up to the roof

---

[287] Homily at a Diocesan Meeting of Catechists, March 10, 2012.

terrace every day, hoping to see him coming back—that good-for-nothing son, no better than a thief for wasting so much, dragging his virtue through the mud. The father knew his task was to wait for life, however it was—beaten, dirty, sinful, broken—just the way it was. His was to wait for that life and welcome it with a father's embrace.

Sometimes we protect ourselves by creating distances, by being very proper, like the scribes and Pharisees: *"I'll have nothing to do with him until he puts his life in order."* They washed their hands a thousand times before eating, and they performed other rituals, but Jesus reproached them for it because their hearts were far from what God wanted—that God who sent His Son to live His life with us, with the least of us.

Those were the friends of Jesus, the least in society. But He took life as He found it. He let men and women be in charge of their own lives, and He accompanied those lives with affection, tenderness, teaching and counsel. He never imposed.

Life is not imposed. Life is planted and watered, not imposed. Everyone is in charge of his or her own life, and God respects this. We are to accompany life the same way God does.

Now back to that father who saw his son coming and was moved to great pity, who was able to feel for this wreck of a man who was his son, a starving vagrant, broken in body and soul. When we think of it, he could have said, "This good-for-nothing took off with all my money, lost it—and now he's back? Did he come back because he's hungry? Let the foreman take care of this, put him to work so he can make up for what he did. Then I'll decide if I want to meet with him." He could have said this, but the father didn't "accompany life" that way. His heart melted and he ran out to hug his son. And when his son begged forgiveness, he calmed his son's weeping with a father's embrace.

Accompany life with the heart of a father and brother. "I don't know what you've done, how you've wasted your life, but I know you're my brother and I have a message from Jesus for you."

The other son in the Gospel story is all self-righteousness, just like the scribes and Pharisees—"I'm pure, I'm always in Church, I belong to a movement, I'm a catechist ... I thank you, Lord, that I am not like the rest of men, like this sinner."

That son closed his heart and preferred hypocritical censoriousness to the tenderness taught him by his father. He didn't know how to accompany life. Probably the most life he could pass on was biological. But never the life that comes from the heart.

And then a great feast was held! Life and encounter are a feast. "Accompanying life" means having the courage to encounter the other as he is, as she is, when they look for me, or I look for them. Accompanying life is an encounter, a festive encounter. Jesus has already told us: *There will be great rejoicing for every one whom you abandon but who comes back, who comes home.* That's encounter!

Here's my question: Among you catechists, are there celebrations? Is there encounter? Or is there stern wagging of fingers followed by a "don't," as teachers used to do in the days of Irigoyen.[288] Are there celebrations? Is there encounter? Do you know what a celebration is, or are you mummies?—mummy catechists relying only on the formulas of truths, of

---

[288] Known generally as "Hipólito Irigoyen," Juan Hipólito del Sagrado Corazón de Jesús Irigoyen Alem (1852-1933) was President of Argentina from 1916 to 1922, and again from 1928 to 1930, an era when schools were much stricter than today. (Trans. note)

commandments; without tenderness, without the ability to encounter.

There should be no place among you for "mummy apostles." Please, no! Mummies belong in a museum, where they do much better. Let there be, instead, hearts that are moved by life "wherever it is kicked," hearts that know how to embrace life and tell life who Jesus is.

With Mary, our tender Mother, taking our hand so that we don't lose our way and mummify our hearts, let us accompany life—hand in hand with her.